Workshop on Linguistic and Neurocognitive Resources (LiNCR2020)

Marseille, France
11 – 16 May 2020

Editors:

Emmanuele Chersoni
Barry Devereux
Chu-Ren Huang

ISBN: 978-1-7138-1266-1

Printed from e-media with permission by:

Curran Associates, Inc.
57 Morehouse Lane
Red Hook, NY 12571

Some format issues inherent in the e-media version may also appear in this print version.

Association for Computational Linguistics
209 N. Eighth Street
Stroudsburg, Pennsylvania 18360

Phone: 1-570-476-8006
Fax: 1-570-476-0860

acl@aclweb.org

Additional copies of this publication are available from:

Curran Associates, Inc.
57 Morehouse Lane
Red Hook, NY 12571 USA
Phone: 845-758-0400
Fax: 845-758-2633
Email: curran@proceedings.com
Web: www.proceedings.com

LREC 2020 Workshop
Language Resources and Evaluation Conference
11–16 May 2020

Workshop on Linguistic and Neurocognitive Resources (LiNCR2020)

PROCEEDINGS

Emmanuele Chersoni, Barry Devereux, Chu-Ren Huang. (eds.)

Proceedings of the LREC 2020 Workshop on Linguistic and Neurocognitive Resources (LiNCr2020)

Editors: Emmanuele Chersoni, Barry Devereux, and Chu-Ren Huang.

For more information:
European Language Resources Association (ELRA)
9 rue des Cordelières
75013, Paris
France
http://www.elra.info
Email: lrec@elda.org

Introduction

In the proceedings of the first LiNCR (pronounced 'linker') workshop in 2018, we stated that the aim of the workshop was to provide a venue to share and explore a new generation of language resources which link and aggregate cognitive, behavioural, neuroimaging and linguistic data. Our vision was to provide a forum for research that leads to the development of methods for the integration of neuro-cognitive data on language function with linguistic facts, the interpretation of experimental data when linked to rich linguistic information, and demonstrations of how new insights can be drawn from this powerful approach in domains such as language learning and neuro-cognitive deficits. We envisioned that there will be many future LiNCR workshops, just as the current 2nd workshop that we are presenting now.

What we did not foresee, however, was that we won't be able to meet face-to-face and strengthen our links during this time of social distancing.

Nevertheless, the eight papers for presentation in this workshop will continue to showcase the innovative nature and potential for impact of this interdisciplinary and data-driven framework for understanding language and cognition. Three significant datasets are presented: the Little Prince corpus for neuro-cognitive studies in 26 languages, sensorimotor norms for Russian, and a dataset for complex emotion learning. Three papers focus on leveraging neuro-cognitive measurement for language technology, or vice versa. Finally, two papers deal with practical issues, such as fonts for dyslexia readers and language models for cloze task answer generation. The eclectic nature of these paper underlines both the vast frontiers to be explored yet as well as the versatility of linked linguistic and neuro-cognitive resources.

Most of all, we look forward to the third LiNCR to update our new findings, to overcome the temporary physical distances, and possibly even to show how linked linguistic and neuro-cognitive databases can shed light on issues related to epidemiology and public health.

Emmanuele Chersoni, Barry Devereux, and Chu-Ren Huang

May 2020

Organizers:

Emmanuele Chersoni (The Hong Kong Polytechnic University)
Barry Devereux (Queen's University Belfast)
Chu-Ren Huang (The Hong Kong Polytechnic University)

Program Committee:

Kathleen Ahrens (The Hong Kong Polytechnic University)
Amir Bakarov (Higher School of Economics, Moscow)
Leonor Becerra-Bonache (Jean Monnet University)
Philippe Blache (LPL-CNRS)
Zhenguang Cai (Chinese University of Hong Kong)
Cristopher Cieri (University of Pennsylvania)
Steven Derby (Queen's University Belfast)
Vesna Djokic (Goldsmiths University of London)
Stefan Frank (Radboud University of Nijmegen)
Diego Frassinelli (University of Stuttgart)
Francesca Frontini (Paul Valéry University of Montpellier)
John Hale (University of Georgia)
Nora Hollenstein (ETH Zurich)
Shu-Kai Hsieh (National Taiwan University)
Yu-Yin Hsu (The Hong Kong Polytechnic University)
Elisabetta Jezek (University of Pavia)
María Dolores Jiménez López (Universitat Rovira i Virgili, Tarragona)
Ping Li (The Hong Kong Polytechnic University)
Andreas Maria Liesenfeld (The Hong Kong Polytechnic University)
Yunfei Long (University of Nottingham)
Brian MacWhinney (Carnegie Mellon University)
Helen Meng (Chinese University of Hong Kong)
Karl David Neergaard (University of Macau)
Noel Nguyen (LPL-CNRS)
Mark Ormerod (Queen's University Belfast)
Christophe Pallier (INSERM-CEA)
Ludovica Pannitto (University of Trento)
Adam Pease (Articulate Software)
Massimo Poesio (Queen Mary University of London)
Stephen Politzer-Ahles (The Hong Kong Polytechnic University)
James Pustejovsky (Brandeis University)
Giulia Rambelli (University of Pisa)
Anna Rogers (University of Massachussetts Lowell)
Marco Senaldi (Scuola Normale Superiore, Pisa)
Adrià Torrens Urrutia (Universitat Rovira i Virgili, Tarragona)
Marten Van Schijndel (Cornell University)
Cory Shain (Ohio State University)
Mingyu Wan (The Hong Kong Polytechnic University)

Table of Contents

Workshop on Linguistic and Neurocognitive Resources (LiNCr2020), pages 1–8
Language Resources and Evaluation Conference (LREC 2020), Marseille, 11–16 May 2020

Extrapolating Binder Style Word Embeddings to New Words

Jacob Turton[1], David Vinson[2], Robert Elliott Smith[1]
[1]Department of Computer Science, University College London
Gower St, London, WC1 EBT
{J.Turton, Rob.Smith}@cs.ucl.ac.uk
[2]Division of Psychology and Language Sciences, University College London
26 Bedford Way, London, WC1H 0AP
d.vinson@ucl.ac.uk

Abstract

Word embeddings such as Word2Vec not only uniquely identify words but also encode important semantic information about them. However, as single entities they are difficult to interpret and their individual dimensions do not have obvious meanings. A more intuitive and interpretable feature space based on neural representations of words was presented by Binder and colleagues (2016) but is only available for a very limited vocabulary. Previous research (Utsumi, 2018) indicates that Binder features can be predicted for words from their embedding vectors (such as Word2Vec), but only looked at the original Binder vocabulary. This paper aimed to demonstrate that Binder features can effectively be predicted for a large number of new words and that the predicted values are sensible. The results supported this, showing that correlations between predicted feature values were consistent with those in the original Binder dataset. Additionally, vectors of predicted values performed comparatively to established embedding models in tests of word-pair semantic similarity. Being able to predict Binder feature space vectors for any number of new words opens up many uses not possible with the original vocabulary size.

Keywords: Semantics, Word-Embeddings, Interpretation

1. Introduction

One of the biggest challenges in computational linguistics is finding representations of words that not only uniquely identify them, but also capture their semantic qualities. A popular approach is distributional semantics (Boleda, 2020), based on the assumption that "a word is characterised by the company it keeps" (Firth, 1957). In practice this means using the co-occurrences of words in large text corpora to derive word embeddings that represent their semantic meaning (Boleda, 2020). Utilising computers makes calculating word co-occurrences in large corpora trivial.

Matrix factorisation approaches such as Latent Semantic Analysis (Landauer et al, 2011) create a term-document matrix and from this produce embeddings for individual words. Alternative matrices can represent term-term co-occurrences or how often words co-occur in sliding window contexts, as is used in the Hyperspace Analogue to Language (HAL) model (Lund & Burgess, 1996).

More recently, models using neural network architectures have proven effective for creating word embeddings. Word2Vec (Mikolov et al, 2013) and GloVe (Pennington. Socher & Manning, 2014) both create word embeddings (typically 300 dimensional) which achieved state of the art results in semantic tasks at their time of introduction. These models are unsupervised; they learn the embeddings from raw text data.

To improve the embeddings, some researchers have proposed infusing them with additional explicit human semantic knowledge. This has resulted in models such as Numberbatch (Speer, Chin & Havasi, 2017), which retrofit the embeddings with information from human created semantic networks, achieving state of the art results in some tests of semantic meaning (e.g. Speer & Lowry-Duda, 2017).

A major difficulty with all word embedding models is interpreting the vectors and validating the semantic information that they capture. By mapping words into a vector space, the relative distance between the embeddings can be used to indicate semantic similarity (Schnabel et al, 2015). This allows word vectors to be understood in terms of their position in vector space in relation to other vectors, but as individual objects in isolation they are difficult to interpret. Furthermore, they offer little insight into *how* the words are related, just that certain words are semantically similar due to their proximity.

This paper proposes mapping word embeddings into a more interpretable feature space, based on the core semantic features of words (Binder et al, 2016). Unfortunately, this feature space currently only exists for a small 535 word vocabulary seriously limiting its uses. Whilst previous work (Utsumi, 2018) has shown that it is possible to derive these feature vectors from embeddings such as Word2Vec, it is still not known how well this scales to a large number of new words. Three experiments were carried out, the first demonstrating that Binder features can be predicted from word embeddings, the second showing that these predictions are sensible for large new word-sets and the third evaluating the performance of the new embeddings in semantic tasks.

By demonstrating that Binder features can be derived for any number of new words, this paper hopes to establish it as a legitimate embedding space.

2. Related Work

2.1 Word Embeddings

Word2Vec, Glove and Numberbatch all represent words as vectors. Word2Vec uses a simple neural network to predict which words should co-occur in a rolling window context. Glove embeddings are derived from a global word co-occurrence matrix. Glove embeddings have been shown to slightly outperform Word2Vec embeddings on certain semantic tasks (Pennington. Socher & Manning, 2014). Numberbatch combines both Word2Vec and GloVe embeddings with information from a semantic network to create a final ensemble embedding for each word. It uses ConceptNet (Speer, Chin & Havasi, 2017) a human created semantic network to inject human level semantic information into the embeddings. To do this it uses a process called retrofitting whereby the vectors of words connected in the semantic network are pushed closer whilst still remaining as close as possible to their original values.

2.2 Interpreting Embeddings

There have been a number of attempts to improve the interpretability of word embeddings. Dimensionality reduction techniques such as Principle Component Analysis (PCA) or t-Distributed Neighbour Stochastic Embedding (t-SNE) allow the high dimensional embeddings to be visualised in lower two or three dimensional spaces (Liu et al, 2017). Word embeddings can then be interpreted in terms of which other words are visually close to them; a human friendly method of interpretation.

Alternatively, clustering methods can be used to group words according to their distances in vector space. The embeddings can then be interpreted in terms of the clusters created (Zhai, Tan & Choi, 2015).

The methods mentioned so far rely on the location of word embeddings in their vector space and their relative distance to other embeddings for them to be interpretable. Other methods try to make the embeddings more interpretable in themselves. Senel et al (2018) identified 110 semantic categories of words and developed word embeddings represented as weightings across these categories. Whilst this allowed embeddings to be interpreted in isolation, each embedding was now being interpreted in relation to other 'complex concepts'; the categories.

This actually relates to a larger issue in semantics, revolving around how words and concepts are defined. A common belief in cognitive linguistics is that people define concepts in terms of their constituent features (e.g. Cree and McRae, 2003). However, these features themselves are often complex concepts which must be defined in terms of yet more features (Binder et al, 2016). This makes defining a concept difficult and, even more troublingly, can result in circular definitions where concepts are defined in terms of each other. Whilst efforts have been made to identify a set of *primitives*: core irreducible features of meaning, results have been mixed (Drobnak, 2009).

2.3 Reflecting Human Semantic Understanding

Binder et al (2016) proposed an alternative method of defining concepts in terms of a core set of semantic features. In a meta-study, they identified 65 semantic features all thought to have specific neural correlates within the brain. The features were chosen to represent different types of meaning in relation to concepts, from visual, to auditory, to tactile and emotional. They then asked human participants to rate a collection of words across this feature set with scores from 0-5. For example when asked to rate a word for the feature 'Vision', participants were asked: 'To what degree is it something you can easily see?'. The authors collected scores for 535 words; 434 nouns, 62 verbs and 39 adjectives. They also made efforts to include words relating to abstract entities as well as concrete objects. Table 1 below gives an example of the mean scores for Vision, Motion and Time features for the first three words in the Binder dataset.

Word	Vision	Motion	Time	Pleasant	Angry
mosquito	2.9	3.6	0.3	0.2	2.9
ire	1.1	0.6	0.2	0.1	5.0
raspberry	4.6	0.0	0.5	4.1	0.2

Table 1: Example semantic feature scores (5 of 65) for three words from Binder et al (2016)

The features that Binder and colleagues proposed are an attractive embedding space as it allows words to be interpreted individually. Moreover, since each dimension is interpretable, *how* words relate or differ can be seen. Binder et al demonstrated that this could be used to differentiate words based on categories, either narrow e.g. mammals vs fish, or more broad e.g. concrete vs abstract. Moreover, they identified a number of important uses for their feature space, including identifying feature importances, representing how abstract concepts are experienced and understanding how concepts can be combined.

However, for the feature space to be useful it needs to cover a decent proportion of the English vocabulary and they only collected ratings for 535 words. Collecting human ratings for even a moderate coverage of the English vocabulary would be prohibitively expensive and time consuming. Instead, it may be possible to predict the feature scores using word embeddings. Abnar et al (2018) demonstrated that word embeddings could be used to predict neural activation associated with concrete nouns. Since the Binder features are intended to relate to specific neural correlates, the embeddings should be able to be used to predict them. In this direction, Utsumi (2018) demonstrated that Binder feature vectors could successfully be derived from word embeddings including Word2Vec and GloVe for words within the Binder dataset. Taking this further and demonstrating that the features can extrapolated to any number of new words with embeddings would massively expand the feature space vocabulary. Previous studies have shown that it is possible to extrapolate feature scores for new words using distributional embeddings (e.g. Mandera, Kueleers & Brysbaert, 2015) albeit for much smaller feature sets.

3. Experiment 1: Predicting Semantic Features

3.1 Introduction

The purpose of this first experiment was to determine whether the values of the 65 semantic features from Binder et al (2016) could be derived from word embeddings in line with Utsumi (2018). A wider range of regression models (five) were tested plus the previously untested Numberbatch embeddings were included. As Numberbatch embeddings combine both GloVe and Word2Vec and include extra human semantic knowledge, it is expected that they should perform best.

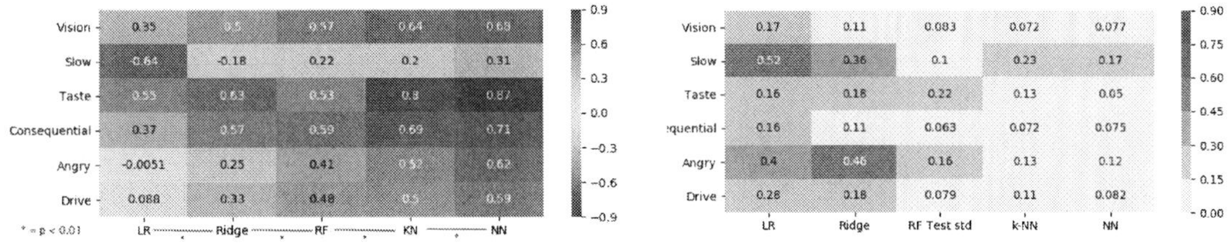

Figure 1: Mean (left) and standard deviation (right) of R-squared scores for six of the 65 Binder semantic features across the 100 test sets. Different models are compared horizontally

3.2 Data

Scores for 535 words across the 65 semantic features were retrieved from Binder et al (2016). Pre-trained Word2Vec (Google, 2013), GloVe (Pennington, Socher & Manning, 2014) and Numberbatch (Speer, Chin & Havasi, 2017) embeddings (all 300 dimensional) were retrieved from their respective online sources. Numberbatch retrofits Word2Vec and GloVe embeddings with information from the ConceptNet knowledge-base.

3.3 Method

Five different types of regression model were compared using GloVe embeddings: linear regressor (LR), ridge regressor (Ridge), random forest regressor (RF), k-nearest neighbours regressor (k-NN) and a 4-layer neural network regressor (NN). Each word in the dataset had a value between 0-5 for each of the 65 semantic features and a 300 dimensional word embedding. The word embeddings were fed into the models as the independent variables with the semantic features as the dependent variables. Separate regression models were trained for each of the features.

For evaluation, models were trained on a subset of the data and their predictions evaluated on a hold-out test set. Because the dataset was fairly small, especially in relation to the number of independent variables (300), there was a risk of overfitting and therefore it was important to maximise the training set size. However, having a test set too small may not appropriately test the models across a representative sample. Utsumi (2018) tackled this using leave-one-out cross validation. In this paper, a bootstrapping method was used instead. 95% of the data was committed for training, and the remaining 5% for testing, but it was repeated over 100 randomly selected train-test set splits. This allowed a large training set whilst testing over a large representative sample of the words overall. The mean and standard deviation of the results could be calculated across the 100 test sets and this also allowed significance testing to compare the model. To ensure fairness, all models were evaluated on the same random 100 train-test splits.

The three different types of word embeddings: Word2Vec, GloVe and Numberbatch were compared using the same method as above.

R-squared was used as the evaluation metric as it was the most intuitive to understand. A Wilcoxon Ranks-sums test was carried out (recommended by Demsar, 2006) to compare the performance of the different models and embeddings.

3.4 Results

Figure 1 above gives the mean R-squared and standard deviations across and six of the 65 features for test set. The six features chosen for Figure 1 represent a mix of concrete and more abstract Binder features.

Table 2 gives the overall mean and standard deviation of test set R-squared scores for each model.

Model	Mean R-sq.	Sd.
Linear Regression	0.03	0.35
Ridge	0.29	0.22
Random Forest	0.41	**0.10**
k-Nearest Neighbours	0.51	0.13
Neural Network	**0.61**	0.11

Table 2: Mean and standard deviation of R-squared scores across all semantic features for the different models.

Table 3 below gives the mean and standard deviation of test set R-squared scores for the different embedding types using the neural network model (best performing model).

Embedding	Mean R-sq.	Sd.
Word2Vec	0.60	0.12
GloVe	0.61	0.10
Numberbatch	**0.65**	**0.09**

Table 3: Overall R-squared mean and standard deviation of different word embeddings

3.5 Discussion

The aim of this experiment was to determine whether semantic feature values from Binder et al (2016) could be derived from word embeddings. In line with the results from Utsumi (2018), this was fairly successful with the best model (Neural Network) achieving an average R-squared of 0.61 across the semantic features, with some features up to ~0.8. Like Utsumi found, there was quite a lot of variation in how well the feature values were predicted, with some such as 'Slow' achieving a relatively low average R-squared (~0.3). Like Utsumi, certain groups of features tended to perform better than others. For example, sensorimotor features such as Toward and Away were more poorly predicted from the embeddings.

However, overall this suggests that for many features a substantial proportion of the variance in human ratings can be derived from word embeddings.

The Neural Network model was the best performing overall, significantly better ($p<0.01$) than the next best performing (k-NN). It was also more consistent than the k-NN model, achieving a lower standard deviation for the features on average. The linear regression model's poor performance may have been due to overfitting as the Ridge regression performed significantly better ($p<0.01$).

Of the word embeddings, Numberbatch (not previously tested in the Utsumi paper) performed the best (0.65), significantly better than both Word2Vec and GloVe ($p<0.01$ for both). This is perhaps not surprising as Numberbatch encourages words connected in a knowledge graph to have similar vectors, and these words will likely also share semantic features.

4. Experiment 2: Predicting Semantic Features for a Larger Vocabulary

4.1 Introduction

Experiment 1 demonstrated that Binder et al (2016) style semantic features could be predicted from word embeddings (albeit with varying success across the features). However, for this to be useful, it is important that the features can be predicted for a much larger vocabulary. Unfortunately, ground truth human ratings for the 65 features only exist for the small Binder et al (2016) dataset, which makes evaluating the predicted scores for new words difficult. Having human scorers evaluate the predicted feature values for new words would be slow and expensive.

One way to overcome this would be to look at the correlations between the semantic features in the human rated Binder dataset and check that they remain consistent for predicted values in a much larger dataset. Binder et al (2016) demonstrated that certain semantic features tended to correlate with each-other across words in their word-set. This pattern of correlations between features should remain consistent within a much larger word-set. Therefore, predicting the semantic values from word embeddings for a new larger word-set of previously unseen words, should give the same or very similar pattern of correlation between the semantic features if the predicted values as sensible.

However, what if the Binder word-set is not a good representation of the wider English vocabulary? As mentioned in the introduction the vast majority of words in the Binder set are nouns, with relatively few verbs or adjectives. The between feature correlations may remain consistent but the predicted semantic values may not be sensible when expanding to a larger new wordset with greater variety of words. Fortunately, much larger datasets of human rated words do exist, but for a much smaller (and slightly different) set of semantic features. The Lancaster Sensorimotor norms (LSN) (Lynott et al, 2019) is a dataset of nearly 40,000 words rated across 11 features by human participants. Some of the features such as *Vision* and *Taste* are very close to features from Binder et al (2016) and all of the words from Binder dataset are included in the larger LSN dataset.

Using the Binder word-set which has human ratings for all of the 65 Binder features and 11 LSN features, the correlations between the LSN and Binder features can be calculated. Then, if the Binder Semantic features are predicted for the larger LSN word-set, it can be checked whether these correlations remain consistent with the LSN features. Since human ratings exist for the 11 LSN features in this larger word-set, it 'grounds' the results. If the pattern of correlations remains consistent, it suggests that the predicted semantic feature values for the new words are sensible.

4.2 Data

The LSN dataset (Lynott et al, 2019) was obtained from their online repository. It consists of 39,707 words rated along 11 features between 0-3.

Numberbatch word embeddings and the Binder et al (2016) dataset from experiment 1 were used again.

4.3 Method

First, the Pearson's correlation was calculated between all 65 semantic features in the Binder et al (2016) dataset, creating a 65×65 correlation matrix. Using the neural network regression model trained in experiment 1 and using Numberbatch embeddings, values for the 65 Binder semantic features across the 39,707 words in the LSN dataset were predicted. The Pearson's correlation between the predicted 65 semantic features across these new words (excluding those also present in the Binder word-set) was calculated, creating another 65×65 correlation matrix. As a numerical measure of similarity, each of the 65 Binder semantic features was represented as a 65 dimensional vector of correlations to all other features, including itself (its row in the correlation matrix). For each feature, the cosine similarity was measured between its correlation vector from the Binder word-set and LSN word-set (ie. 'Vision' Binder vector and 'Vision' LSN vector). Under perfect circumstances, the similarity would be 1 indicating identical vectors. For comparison, cosine similarity of correlation vectors for mismatched features from the Binder and LSN word-set were calculated (e.g. 'Vision' and 'Shape'). It would be expected that these would give a cosine similarity much lower than 1.

The same procedure as above was used for comparing the 11 LSN features to the 65 Binder features. Each of the 11 LSN features was represented as a 65 dimensional vector of correlations with the 65 Binder features. For each feature the cosine similarity between their vectors from the Binder and LSN dataset were calculated. For comparison, the cosine similarity between each of the 11 LSN feature's correlation vectors from the Binder dataset and every other feature's LSN dataset vectors were calculated.

Additionally, a correlation heat-map was created between the features for the Binder and LSN word-sets each separately and then plotted for visual inspection.

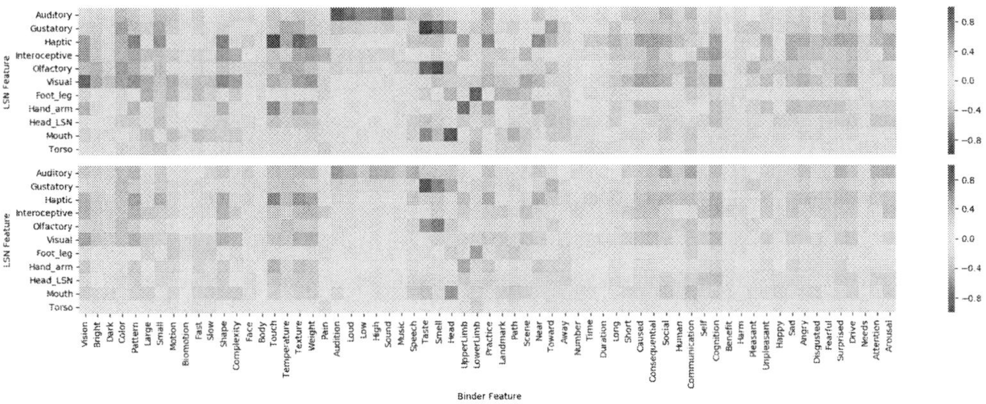

Figure 2: Correlations between the 11 LSN features and 65 Binder semantic features for the Binder word-set (top) and LSN word-set (bottom)

4.4 Results

Table 4 below gives the mean cosine similarity between the same feature correlation vectors from the Binder and LSN word-sets and between different feature vectors.

	Cosine Sim Mean	Cosine Sim S.d.
Same Feature	**0.985**	0.008
Different Features	0.063	0.490

Table 4: Binder semantic feature correlation vector cosine similarities between the Binder and LSN word-sets

Figure 2 above gives the heat-maps for correlations between the 11 LSN features and 65 Binder features for the Binder word-set (top) and LSN word-set (bottom).

4.5 Results

Table 4 below gives the mean cosine similarity between the same feature correlation vectors from the Binder and LSN word-sets and between different feature vectors.

	Cosine Sim Mean	Cosine Sim S.d.
Same Feature	**0.985**	0.008
Different Features	0.063	0.490

Table 4: Binder semantic feature correlation vector cosine similarities between the Binder and LSN word-sets

Figure 2 above gives the heat-maps for correlations between the 11 LSN features and 65 Binder features for the Binder word-set (top) and LSN word-set (bottom).

Table 5 gives the mean cosine similarity of LSN feature correlation vectors between the Binder and LSN word-sets.

	Cosine Sim Mean	Cosine Sim S.d.
Same Feature	**0.94**	0.04
Different Features	-0.02	0.56

Table 5: LSN feature correlation vector cosine similarities between the Binder and LSN word-sets

4.6 Discussion

Table 4 shows that the mean cosine similarity is very high (almost 1) for correlation vectors of the same semantic feature in the Binder and LSN word-sets. This is compared to the very low (almost 0) cosine similarity between the correlation vectors of different features from the Binder and LSN word-sets. This demonstrates that the patterns of correlations between the 65 Binder features remained fairly consistent in the larger LSN word-set where the values had been predicted using the neural network model.

For the 11 LSN features, the heat-maps show a similar pattern of correlations for the features between the Binder and LSN word-sets. The colours are slightly less intense in the LSN word-set suggesting the correlations are slightly weaker. However, this would be expected due to noise from errors in predicting the feature values. The mean cosine similarity is very high (nearly 1) for feature correlation vectors matched across the Binder and LSN word-sets and almost 0 for non-matching features.

Together these results suggest that the values predicted for the 65 semantic features from word embeddings are sensible even in a large and diverse new vocabulary such as the LSN word-set.

5. Experiment 3: Validation of the New Feature Space

5.1 Introduction

Experiments 1 and 2 demonstrated that the values of 65 semantic features could be successfully predicted from word embeddings, and that these appear to be consistent across a large vocabulary of previously unseen words.

Whilst this new feature space is not intended to replace existing embeddings (in fact since it is purely derived from them it almost certainly contains less information about the words) it is still important to demonstrate that it does capture sufficient semantic information.

One of the most common methods for validating word embeddings is using semantic similarity datasets. Typically, these datasets contain pairs of words which are

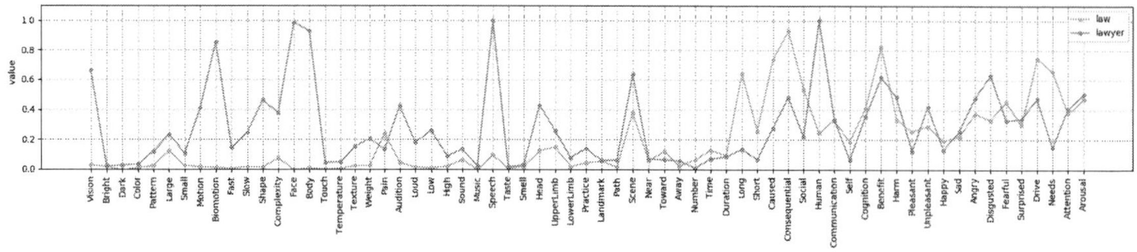

Figure 3: Predicted Semantic Features of words 'law' and 'lawyer'

rated for semantic similarity by human participants. Cosine similarity between word embeddings can be used as a measure of their semantic similarity according to the embedding model. Well performing models should give cosine similarities between words in the pairs that correlate closely to the human ratings.

In the Binder feature space, each word can be represented as a 65 dimensional vector with a value for each of the semantic features. For new words, these vectors can be created by predicting the values for each of the semantic features, similar to in experiments 1 and 2. The cosine similarity between these vectors can then be calculated as a measure of semantic similarity. The aim of this final experiment was to validate the similarity measurements between the predicted vectors against human ratings of similarity.

5.2 Data

Three different word similarity datasets were used: Wordsim-353 (Gabrilovich, 2002), Simlex-999 (Hill, Reichart & Korhonen, 2015) and Verbsim (Yang and Powers, 2006). The same pre-trained Word2Vec, Numberbatch and GloVe embeddings as experiment 1 were used. The same neural network trained on the Binder et al (2016) dataset as experiments 1 & 2 was used.

5.3 Method

A vocabulary was created consisting of all words from the three similarity datasets. Using the trained neural network model and the Numberbatch vectors for the words, values for the 65 semantic features were predicted for the words in the vocabulary. This resulted in a 65 dimensional vector for each of the words, where for each word each dimension was the value of each semantic feature for that word.

For each of the similarity datasets, the cosine similarity was calculated between the semantic feature vectors of the words in each pair. The cosine similarity was also calculated for the Word2Vec, GloVe and Numberbatch embeddings as a comparison.

Spearman's rank correlation was used as it compares the similarity rankings of the word pairs between the human ratings and the ratings derived from the embeddings.

5.4 Results

Table 6 below gives the Spearman's rank coefficient between the word embedding cosine similarity ratings and the ground truth human ratings across the three different word pair datasets.

Embeddings	WordSim353	SimLex999	SimVerb
Word2Vec	0.69	0.44	0.36
GloVe	0.72	0.41	0.28
Numberbatch	**0.83**	**0.63**	**0.57**
Predicted Binder	0.47	0.54	0.46

Table 6: Spearman's Rank correlation between model and human similarity ratings for different word-pair datasets

Whilst Numberbatch embeddings performed best on all datasets, the predicted feature embeddings performed fairly well, beating Word2Vec and GloVe on two of the three datasets. However, the predicted embeddings performed particularly poorly on the Wordsim-353 dataset, performing the worse by far.

5.5 Discussion

At first, the particularly poor performance of the predicted semantic vectors on the Wordsim-353 dataset seems discouraging. However, the Wordsim dataset has received criticism for containing a high proportion of word pairs rated high in similarity through association (e.g. law and lawyer) rather than pure semantic meaning (Hill et al, 2015). Since the predicted Binder semantic embedding space defines words in terms of semantic features, it is understandable that it would not capture similarity due to association as associated words do not necessarily share core features. The SimLex-999 dataset was specifically designed to avoid word pairs with high ratings due to association. The better performance of the predicted feature embeddings on this dataset indicates that the poor performance on the Wordsim dataset was likely due to these association word pairs.

The performance of the predicted embeddings on the SimVerb dataset is also encouraging seeing as there were relatively few verbs in the Binder et al (2016) dataset used for training the prediction model. And it indicates that the model should be suitable for predicting semantic features for new verbs.

Figure 3 above illustrates how two words with high human rated similarity due to association (law and lawyer) are represented by the predicted feature vectors. I this embedding space it can be seen that they are considered very different. Lawyer appears to be represented as a human concrete object: a person as a professional lawyer. The law on the other hand appears to be a more abstract concept (as indicated by the very low scores across all visual, auditory and sensorimotor features). By these senses the concepts are very different, even though to a human they may seem very similar due to their high association.

Finally, whether word similarity datasets are the best way to evaluate word embedding semantics is debatable. Faruqui et al (2016) provide several shortcomings of word similarity tests for evaluating word embeddings. In light of this, the poorer performance of the Binder embeddings may not mean they do not hold important semantic information

6. General Discussion

The aim of this research was to demonstrate that the Binder semantic feature space for words can be extrapolated to a much larger vocabulary of words using word embeddings. This was important as the Binder word-set is limited to only 535 words.

In line with Utsumi (2018), Experiment 1 demonstrated that Binder features can be derived from word embeddings, with the previously untested Numberbatch embeddings giving the best performance. Like in the Ustumi paper, a neural network architecture model performed best. Experiment 2 demonstrated that the predicted values for a large set of new words appeared sensible, with the internal correlations between the features remaining consistent with human rated words. Finally, experiment 3 showed that this new embedding space retains important semantic information about words, performing comparatively to established embedding models. However, it does not capture associations between words well which may be an important aspect of semantic similarity that it fails on.

The purpose of mapping words to this new feature space is not to replace existing embedding models, but to provide an alternative way to view word embeddings. As Figure 3, on the previous page, illustrates the words represented in this feature space are quite easy to interpret. Furthermore, the semantic features that either differentiate or liken words can easily be identified. The fact that this feature space can be fully derived from existing word embeddings such as Numberbatch, suggests that this semantic information is all present within the word embeddings. However, the range in explained variance between the predicted features does suggest that some semantic information is better captured by word embeddings than other. This is something that Utsumi (2018) investigated in greater detail.

Finally, being able to predict the feature values from existing word embeddings allows the Binder feature space to be extrapolated to a much larger vocabulary. This makes many of the uses for the feature space, outlined in Binder et al (2016), more realistic as their original dataset was too limited in size.

7. Bibliographical References

Abnar, S., Ahmed, R., Mijnheer, M. & Zuidema, W. (2018). Experiential, Distributional and Dependency-based Word Embeddings have Complementary Roles in Decoding Brain Activity, *Proceedings of the 8th Workshop on Cognitive Modeling and Computational Linguistics*, 57-66.

Binder, J. R., Conant, L. L., Humphries, C. J., Fernandino, L., Simons, S. B., Aguilar, M., & Desai, R. H. (2016). Toward a Brain-Based Componential Semantic Representation. *Cognitive neuropsychology*, 33(3-4):130-174.

Boleda, G. (2020). Distributional Semantics and Linguistic Theory. *Annual Review of Linguistics*. 6:213-234

Cree, G. S., & McRae, K. (2003). Analyzing the Factors Underlying the Structure and Computation of the Meaning of Chipmunk, Cherry, Chisel, Cheese, and Cello (and Many Other Such Concrete Nouns). *Journal of experimental psychology: general*, 132(2):163.

Demšar, J. (2006). Statistical Comparisons of Classifiers Over Multiple Data Sets. *Journal of Machine learning research*, 7:1-30.

Drobnak, F. T. (2009). On the Merits and Shortcomings of Semantic Primes and Natural Semantic Metalanguage in Cross-Cultural Translation. *ELOPE: English Language Overseas Perspectives and Enquiries*. 6(1-2):29-41.

Faruqui, M., Tsvetkov, Y., Rastogi, P. & Dyer, C. (2016) Problems With Evaluation of Word Embeddings Using Word Similarity Tasks, *Proceedings of the 1st Workshop on Evaluating Vector-Space Representations for NLP*. 30-35

Firth, J.R. (1957). Applications of General Linguistics, *Transactions of the Philological Society*. 56(1):1-14

Landauer, T. K., McNamara, D. S., Dennis, S., & Kintsch, W. (Eds.). (2013). *Handbook of latent semantic analysis*. Psychology Press. New York.

Liu, S., Bremer, P. T., Thiagarajan, J. J., Srikumar, V., Wang, B., Livnat, Y., & Pascucci, V. (2017). Visual Exploration of Semantic Relationships in Neural Word Embeddings. *IEEE transactions on visualization and computer graphics*, 24(1):553-562.

Lund, K., & Burgess, C. (1996). Producing High-Dimensional Semantic Spaces from Lexical Co-occurrence. *Behavior research methods, instruments, & computers*, 28(2):203-208.

Lynott, D., Connell, L., Brysbaert, M., Brand, J., & Carney, J. (2019). The Lancaster Sensorimotor Norms: Multidimensional Measures of Perceptual and Action Strength for 40,000 English Words. *Behavior Research Methods*, 1-21.

Mikolov, T., Chen, K., Corrado, G., & Dean, J. (2013). Efficient Estimation of Word Representations in Vector Space. *arXiv preprint*. ArXiv:1301.3781

Mandera, P., Keuleers, E., & Brysbaert, M. (2015). How Useful are Corpus-Based Methods for Extrapolating Psycholinguistic Variables?. *The Quarterly Journal of Experimental Psychology*. 68(8):1623-1642.

Pennington, J., Socher, R., & Manning, C. D. (2014). Glove: Global Vectors for Word Representation. *In Proceedings of the 2014 conference on empirical methods in natural language processing (EMNLP)*. Pages 1532-1543.

Schnabel, T., Labutov, I., Mimno, D., & Joachims, T. (2015, September). Evaluation Methods for Unsupervised Word Embeddings. *In Proceedings of the 2015 conference on empirical methods in natural language processing*. Pages 298-307.

Şenel, L. K., Utlu, I., Yücesoy, V., Koc, A., & Cukur, T. (2018). Semantic Structure and Interpretability of Word Embeddings. *IEEE/ACM Transactions on Audio, Speech, and Language Processing*, 26(10):1769-1779.

Speer, R., Chin, J., & Havasi, C. (2017, February). Conceptnet 5.5: An Open Multilingual Graph of General Knowledge. *In Thirty-First AAAI Conference on Artificial Intelligence*.

Speer, R., & Lowry-Duda, J. (2017). Conceptnet at Semeval-2017 Task 2: Extending Word Embeddings With Multilingual Relational Knowledge. *arXiv preprint arXiv*:1704.03560.

Utsumi, A. (2018). A Neurobiologically Motivated Analysis of Distributional Semantic Models. *Proceedings of the 40th Annual Conference of the Cognitive Science Society*, 1147-1152.

Zhai, M., Tan, J., & Choi, J. D. (2016, March). Intrinsic and Extrinsic Evaluations of Word Embeddings. *In Thirtieth AAAI Conference on Artificial Intelligence*.

8. Language Resource References

Hill, F., Reichart, R. & Korhonen, A. (2015). SimLex-999: Evaluating Semantic Models with (Genuine) Similarity Estimation. *Computational Linguistics*. https://fh295.github.io/simlex.html

Gabrivolvich, E. (2002). The WordSimilairty-353 Test Collection. http://www.cs.technion.ac.il/~gabr/resources/data/wordsim353/

Google. (2013). Google Code Archive, Word2Vec. https://code.google.com/archive/p/word2vec/

Pennington, J., Socher, R., & Manning, C. D. (2014). Glove: Global Vectors for Word Representation. *In Proceedings of the 2014 conference on empirical methods in natural language processing (EMNLP)*. https://nlp.stanford.edu/projects/glove/

Speer, R., Chin, J., & Havasi, C. (2017, February). Conceptnet 5.5: An Open Multilingual Graph of General Knowledge. *In Thirty-First AAAI Conference on Artificia Intelligence*. https://github.com/commonsense/conceptnet-numberbatch

Yang, D. & Powers, D. M. (2006). *Verb Similarity on the Taxonomy of WordNet*. Masaryk University.

Workshop on Linguistic and Neurocognitive Resources (LiNCr2020), pages 9–14
Language Resources and Evaluation Conference (LREC 2020), Marseille, 11–16 May 2020

Towards the First Dyslexic Font in Russian

Svetlana Alexeeva, Aleksandra Dobrego, Vladislav Zubov
St. Petersburg State University, University of Helsinki, St. Petersburg State University
Universitetskaya emb. 7/9, 199034, Saint-Petersburg, Russia
Yliopistonkatu 4, 00100, Helsinki, Finland
mail@s-alexeeva.ru, alexandra.dobrego@gmail.com, vladzubov21@gmail.com

Abstract

Texts comprise a large part of visual information that we process every day, so one of the tasks of language science is to make them more accessible. However, often the text design process is focused on the font size, but not on its type; which might be crucial especially for the people with reading disabilities. The current paper represents a study on text accessibility and the first attempt to create a research-based accessible font for Cyrillic letters. This resulted in the dyslexic-specific font, LexiaD. Its design rests on the reduction of inter-letter similarity of the Russian alphabet. In evaluation stage, dyslexic and non-dyslexic children were asked to read sentences from the Children version of the Russian Sentence Corpus. We tested the readability of LexiaD compared to PT Sans and PT Serif fonts. The results showed that all children had some advantage in letter feature extraction and information integration while reading in LexiaD, but lexical access was improved when sentences were rendered in PT Sans or PT Serif. Therefore, in several aspects, LexiaD proved to be faster to read and could be recommended to use by dyslexics who have visual deficiency or those who struggle with text understanding resulting in re-reading.

Keywords: dyslexia, font, eye movements

1. Introduction

1.1 Dyslexia

Dyslexia is one of the most common reading disabilities in children. Some estimations show the incidence of dyslexia to be 4-10% (Castles et al., 2010). In Russia, 5-10% of children suffer from dyslexia (Kornev, 2003).

Most definitions of dyslexia fall into two approaches: pedagogical and clinical/psychological. In this paper, we follow the second approach, meaning that dyslexia is a persistent, selective inability to master reading skills in the presence of optimal learning conditions, despite a sufficient level of intellectual development and no impairments of auditory or visual analyzers (Kornev, 2003).

One of the theories trying to explain this phenomenon - the theory of phonological deficit in reading - is associated with the lack of formation of speech processes (Ramus et al., 2003). In this case, the problem of mastering the skill of sound-letter reading is due to the inability of the child to establish a link between the auditory and self-spoken speech, and, accordingly, between oral speech and writing. In turn, the theory of visual deficiency in reading explains dyslexia by dysfunction of the visual system (Stein & Walsh, 1997), which is responsible for visual recognition and controls eye movements (Stein, 2018). Dyslexics indicate the following problems in reading: letters in the words change places or are blurred, and the lines of the text shift. Studies indicate that oculomotor activity of children with and without dyslexia have quantitative and qualitative differences (Pavlidis, 1981).

In this work, the theory of visual deficiency is of particular interest, since such visual difficulties in reading were not only subjectively described by dyslexics but also objectively proved in some studies (Mueller & Weidemann, 2012). It was shown that a letter in a word is recognized by its distinctive features. Since the distinctive letter elements and text appearance in general depend on the font type, it is an important criterion for identifying letters in the process of reading.

1.2 Fonts

Different types of fonts are divided into groups according to the presence of serifs (serif - Times New Roman, sans serif - Arial) and letter width (monospaced - `Courier`, proportional - Arial). Most research in the field of font readability for Latin alphabet aims to determine which font type is easier to read.

At the moment there is no consensus on whether serifs affect font perception. Some studies show that there is no effect of serifs on font perception (e.g. Perea, 2013), others show that serifs slow down the processes of reading and character recognition since serifs create visual noise that complicates letter identification process (Wilkins et al., 2007). However, sans serif fonts are agreed to be recognized faster (Woods et al., 2005). The advantage of sans serif font is also noted in the study (Lidwell et al., 2010), which demonstrated that the absence of serifs increases text readability for participants with reading disabilities.

Although there are quite few works looking at serifs, studies comparing monospaced (all letters have the same width) and proportional (width of a letter depends on its geometric shape) fonts are in abundance. Monospaced fonts are known for worsening recognition process, and the recommendations of designers urge to avoid such fonts (Rello & Baeza-Yates, 2013).

Latin alphabet has been studied extensively, which is not the case for Cyrillic letters. One of the studies (Alexeeva & Konina, 2016) presented the participants Courier New letters in two conditions - in isolation and as part of a sequence – and built the first confusion matrix for Russian. Further exploration (Alexeeva et al., 2019) revealed that typeface does influence letter recognition: letters written in proportional Georgia are more intelligible than the ones written in monospaced `Courier New`.

1.2.1 Recommendations

There are barely any font recommendations for people with reading disabilities. The British Dyslexia Association advises to use sans serif fonts (Arial, Comic Sans) and to avoid fancy options (italics, decorative fonts) but doesn't specify reasons of why these fonts are suggested. Sans serif fonts as dyslexic-friendly were also mentioned in (Evett & Brown, 2005; Lockley, 2002).

1.3 The problem and the principle for our solution

Since font influences success of letter recognition inside a word, we assume that a properly designed font will facilitate letter recognition, both for people with normal reading skills and dyslexics.

Although many Latin-based dyslexia-friendly fonts are of frequent use (i.e. Dyslexie, OpenDyslexic, Sylexiad, Read Regular), empirical studies failed to prove that these fonts have any effect on reading for dyslexics (Rello & Baeza-Yates, 2013; Wery & Diliberto, 2017; Kuster et al., 2017). In fact, designers of those fonts were inspired by their own reading difficulties and did not perform any objective inter-letter similarity pretests.

In our project, we made the first attempt to design dyslexia-friendly font for the Russian alphabet. To avoid past mistakes, we developed our font, LexiaD, on the grounds of empirical results. Namely, we conducted a preliminary eye-tracking study where letter confusions were identified. The reduction of inter-letter similarity in LexiaD was the main principle that guided type designers we worked with — M. Golovatyuk and S. Rasskazov.

1.4 LexiaD

The main idea of LexiaD was to make all letters as dissimilar as possible, following the previous study (Alexeeva & Konina, 2016). For example, letters т and г that are frequently confused in other fonts were designed as m and ƨ, in a way they are handwritten. Here are the most important LexiaD features:

- It is proportional and sans serif, since it was found that serifs and monospace complicate reading (see 1.2 Fonts).
- It is designed for 14 plus pins, since it is more convenient for children with and without dyslexia to work with a larger font (O'Brien et al., 2005; Wilkins et al., 2007).
- The amount of white inside letters and in between varies, and the distance between lines is double line spacing. It was shown that increased distance between letters and words, and an increase in the amount of white facilitates text perception by dyslexics (Zorzi et al., 2012).
- As for the exact features, the designers changed similar elements in the letters, made each letter in the new font as different as possible from the other, but easy to read:
    - "Recognizable clues", emphasizing individual characteristics of letters.
    - Extended letters that help distinguish certain characters from others.
    - Thickening of horizontals and diagonals of letters, which visually distinguishes characters from others.

Figure 1 shows the Russian alphabet rendered in LexiaD.

абвгдеёжзийклмнопрстуфхцчшщъыьэюя
АБВГДЕЁЖЗИЙКЛМНОПРСТУФХЦЧШЩЪЫЬЭЮЯ

Figure 1: The Russian alphabet in LexiaD font

2. Methodology

The purpose of this study is to assess the readability of the first special Cyrillic font LexiaD by dyslexic children and children without dyslexia, specifically, to compare LexiaD to PT Sans and PT Serif - modern open license fonts that were specifically designed to render Russian and other Cyrillic-based alphabets, and are claimed to be one of best sans serif and serif typefaces (Farář, 2011).

Figure 2 shows all three used fonts for the purpose of visual comparison.

LexiaD	Обещают, что лето будет жарким.
PT Sans	Обещают, что лето будет жарким.
PT Serif	Обещают, что лето будет жарким.

Figure 2: An example sentence in LexiaD, PT Sans and PT Serif fonts[1]

Since each letter in LexiaD has its own characteristics and a minimum number of elements similar to other letters, it was assumed that the sentences presented in this font will be read faster than in PT Sans or PT Serif. Also, a number of comprehension errors in LexiaD will be less or equal to that in PT Sans or PT Serif. Readability was tested with an eye-tracker.

2.1 Participants

We recruited 3rd and 4th-grade children with and without dyslexia (9-12 age-old).

Dyslexic children were students of public schools in Moscow (further "PT Sans/LexiaD" part) and St.Petersburg (further "PT Serif/LexiaD" part). Children in Moscow were diagnosed with dyslexia according to the adapted requirements of Neuropsychological Test Battery (Akhutina et al., 2016) by Svetlana Dorofeeva, Center for Language and Brain, HSE Moscow. The Test took about 2 hours to complete, therefore only 6 dyslexics (3 boys) participated in PT Sans/LexiaD part of the study. Children in St. Petersburg were recruited via speech remediation school №3; 31 children (26 boys) participated in PT Serif/LexiaD part.

Non-dyslexic children were students of public school №491. 22 of them (8 boys) participated in PT Sans/LexiaD part, and 25 of them (13 boys) – in the PT Serif/LexiaD part. None of them had any language impairments.

All participants had (a) normal level of intellectual development; (b) normal vision; (c) no comorbid diagnoses (e.g., autism), and (d) were naive to the purpose of the experiment.

2.2 Materials and design

We used the Children version of the Russian Sentence Corpus (Korneev et al., 2018), consisting of 30 sentences (ranged in length from 6 to 9 words, with the total number of 227 words). For each word in the corpus, word frequencies and word length were calculated. Frequencies were determined using a subcorpus of children's texts from 1920 to 2019 of the Russian National Corpus (http://ruscorpora.ru, comprising more than 4 million tokens).

Half of the sentences were presented in PT Sans or PT Serif (depending on the part of the study, see 2.1 Participants)

[1] "They say that summer will be hot"

and the other half – in LexiaD. In the PT Sans/LexiaD part sentences in PT Sans were rendered in 21 pt, and sentences in LexiaD – in 26 pt, whereas in the PT Serif/LexiaD part sizes of 17 pt and 21 pt were used respectively. In both cases the physical height of each font pair was equal. Size differences were due to different distances from a participant to a monitor that depended on the workplace provided.

The order of fonts, order of sentences and distribution of sentences between the fonts were random for each child.

Three practice sentences were presented at the beginning of the experiment. To ensure that participants were paying attention to the task, 33% of the sentences were followed by a two-choice comprehension question; the response was registered by the keyboard. Sentences and questions were typed in black on a white background.

2.3 Equipment

SR Research EyeLink 1000 plus camera mounted eye-tracker was used to record eye movements. The recording of eye movements was carried out in monocular mode, every 1 ms. The experiment was created using the Experiment Builder software developed by SR Research.

2.4 Procedure

Participants were instructed to read the sentences attentively. A head restraint was used to minimize head movements. The initial calibration procedure lasted approximately 5 min, and calibration accuracy was checked prior to every trial in the experiment. After reading each sentence, a participant pressed a key button to continue.

3. Results

3.1 Data analysis

Eye movements are described by fixations and saccades: fixations occur when eyes are relatively stable (and intake of visual information occurs), and saccades — when eyes move rapidly from one text region to another.

In this study, fixations under 80 ms within one character of the next or previous fixation were combined with the respective fixation. Remaining fixations under 80 ms as well as fixations before and after a blink were discarded. The first and last words in every sentence were excluded from the analyses.

Following standard practices in eye movement research (Rayner, 1998), we examined two measures of initial processing time for the corpus words: first-fixation duration (FFD, the duration of the first fixation on a word independent of the number of fixations that were made on the word), gaze duration (GD, the sum of all fixations on a word before moving the eyes off that word), and one measure of late processing: total viewing time (TVT, the sum of all fixations on a word including fixations while re-reading). FFDs and GDs were measured even if a word was at first skipped and then fixated (6% in PT Sans/LexiaD and 7% in the PT Serif/LexiaD. The words that are completely skipped were discarded from the analysis (9% in PT Sans/LexiaD and 8% in the PT Serif/LexiaD).

It is claimed (Liversedge et al., 2011) that earlier reading measures reflect early stages of cognitive processing (e.g. feature extraction and lexical access) whereas effects associated with later stages of processing (e.g. discourse processing and recovering after a syntactic or semantic disruption) affect later reading time measures. It is also believed that optimal fixation location is a center of the word (Nuthmann et al., 2005) as this position makes all or most of the letters clearly visible. Therefore, if a fixation lands far from the center (e.g. due to a motor error), then not all letter visual information will be extracted fully, and most likely a refixation will be made. Therefore, we assume that first fixation duration is primarily related to feature extraction, gaze duration mainly reflects lexical access, and total viewing time captures text integration.

We performed two (generalized) linear mixed effects analyses ((G)LMM) using the lme4 package in R to assess the effect of font and participant group (with / without dyslexia) on each of the eye movement measures (dependent variables) and comprehension accuracy. Controlled effects — word length and word frequencies — and two-way interactions between all factors were included in the analyses. We explored the data from the PT Sans/LexiaD in the first analysis, and the data from the PT Serif/LexiaD — in the second one.

To ensure a normal distribution of model residuals, durations (FFD, GD, and TVT) were log-transformed. Binary dependent variables (accuracy) were fit with GLMMs with a logistic link function. Font and Participant group factors were coded as sliding contrasts (with LexiaD and dyslexics as a reference level, respectively).

The lmerTest package in R was used to estimate the p-values. Step procedure was conducted for optimal model selection. Results for all models are indicated in Tables 1, 2, 3 and 4 below (significant effects are in bold).

<table>
<tr><td></td><td colspan="4">PT Sans / LexiaD</td><td colspan="4">PT Serif / LexiaD</td></tr>
<tr><td colspan="9">First Fixation Duration (FFD)</td></tr>
<tr><td>Optimal model</td><td colspan="4">log(FFD) ~ font + group + log(freq) + (1 + font | subj) + (1 + group | word)</td><td colspan="4">log(FFD) ~ font + log(freq) + length + font:log(freq) + (1 + font | subj) + (1 + group | word)</td></tr>
<tr><td>Predictors</td><td colspan="4">Model estimates</td><td colspan="4">Model estimates</td></tr>
<tr><td></td><td>b</td><td>SE</td><td>t</td><td>p</td><td>b</td><td>SE</td><td>t</td><td>p</td></tr>
<tr><td>Font</td><td>0.06</td><td>0.018</td><td>3.27</td><td>0.003</td><td>0.02</td><td>0.018</td><td>0.97</td><td>0.334</td></tr>
<tr><td>Group</td><td>-0.25</td><td>0.070</td><td>-3.58</td><td>0.001</td><td></td><td></td><td></td><td></td></tr>
<tr><td>Log(freq)</td><td>-0.02</td><td>0.003</td><td>-5.44</td><td><0.001</td><td>-0.02</td><td>0.003</td><td>-7.48</td><td><0.001</td></tr>
<tr><td>Length</td><td></td><td></td><td></td><td></td><td><0.01</td><td>0.003</td><td>-2.54</td><td>0.012</td></tr>
<tr><td>Font:log (freq)</td><td></td><td></td><td></td><td></td><td><0.01</td><td>0.004</td><td>2.43</td><td>0.015</td></tr>
</table>

Table 1: Fixed effect results for first fixation duration.

<table>
<tr><td></td><td colspan="4">PT Sans / LexiaD</td><td colspan="4">PT Serif / LexiaD</td></tr>
<tr><td colspan="9">Gaze Duration (GD)</td></tr>
<tr><td>Optimal model</td><td colspan="4">log(GD) ~ font + group + log(freq) + length + font:log(freq) + (1 + group | word) + (1 | subj) + (1 | trial)</td><td colspan="4">log(GD) ~ font + group + log(freq) + length + font:log(freq) + group:log(freq) + (1 + font | subj) + (1 | word)</td></tr>
<tr><td>Predictors</td><td colspan="4">Model estimates</td><td colspan="4">Model estimates</td></tr>
<tr><td></td><td>b</td><td>SE</td><td>t</td><td>p</td><td>b</td><td>SE</td><td>t</td><td>p</td></tr>
<tr><td>Font</td><td>-0.08</td><td>0.032</td><td>-2.56</td><td>0.010</td><td>-0.05</td><td>0.0241</td><td>-2.18</td><td>0.030</td></tr>
<tr><td>Group</td><td>-0.60</td><td>0.127</td><td>-4.78</td><td><0.001</td><td>- 0.03</td><td>0.098</td><td>-2.74</td><td>0.008</td></tr>
<tr><td>Log(freq)</td><td>-0.05</td><td>0.007</td><td>-7.84</td><td><0.001</td><td>-0.07</td><td>0.006</td><td>-10.81</td><td><0.001</td></tr>
<tr><td>Length</td><td>0.08</td><td>0.008</td><td>9.42</td><td><0.001</td><td>0.07</td><td>7.076e-03</td><td>9.70</td><td><0.001</td></tr>
<tr><td>Font:log (freq)</td><td>0.01</td><td>0.007</td><td>2.09</td><td>0.037</td><td><0.01</td><td>0.005</td><td>1.99</td><td>0.047</td></tr>
<tr><td>Group:log (freq)</td><td></td><td></td><td></td><td></td><td>0.02</td><td>0.005</td><td>4.21</td><td><0.001</td></tr>
</table>

Table 2: Fixed effect results for gaze duration.

	PT Sans / LexiaD				PT Serif / LexiaD			
Total Viewing Time (TVT)								
Optimal model	log(TVT) ~ font + group + log(freq) + length) + font:log(freq) + group:length + (1 + font | subj) + (1 | word) + (1 | trial)				log(TVT) ~ font + group + log(freq) + length + font:lengh + group:length + group:log(freq)+ (1 + font | subj) + (1 | word) + (1 | trial)			
Predictors	*Model estimates*				*Model estimates*			
	b	SE	t	p	b	SE	t	p
Font	-0.07	0.032	-2.10	**0.039**	<0.01	0.037	2.63	**0.009**
Group	-0.06	0.181	-3.08	**0.004**	-0.33	0.118	-2.82	**0.006**
Log(freq)	-0.07	0.008	-8.17	**<0.001**	-0.08	0.008	-9.83	**<0.001**
Length	0.10	<0.001	10.28	**<0.001**	0.08	<0.001	8.52	**<0.001**
Font:log (freq)	0.02	0.006	3.65	**<0.001**				
Font: length					-0.01	0.005	-2.62	**0.009**
Group: Length	-0.05	0.008	-6.71	**<0.001**	-0.02	0.007	-2.62	**0.009**
Group: log (freq)					-0.02	0.006	2.99	**0.003**

Table 3: Fixed effect results for total viewing time.

	PT Sans / LexiaD				PT Serif / LexiaD			
Accuracy (ACC)								
Optimal model	ACC ~ font + group + font:group+ (1 + font | subj) + (1 | trial)				ACC ~ font + group + font:group+ (1 + font | subj) + (1 | trial)			
Predictors	*Model estimates*				*Model estimates*			
	b	SE	z	p	b	SE	z	p
Font	0.81	1.215	0.67	0.503	0.34	0.460	0.74	0.461
Group	0.65	0.824	0.79	0.428	0.05	0.370	0.14	0.885
Font: group	-0.67	1.608	-0.42	0.675	0.02	0.702	0.03	0.978

Table 4: Fixed effect results for accuracy.

3.2 Effects of LexiaD

3.2.1 PT Sans/LexiaD

There was a robust effect of font on FFD: readers fixated longer on words in PT Sans (348 ms) than on words in LexiaD (325 ms).

Effect of font was significant for GD but invertedly: words in LexiaD were fixated at longer (532 ms) than words in PT Sans (491 ms). Also, there was a significant interaction between font and word frequency, meaning the advantage of the LexiaD for high-frequency words and the disadvantage — for low-frequency ones.

For TVT, readers fixated significantly longer on words in LexiaD (676 ms) than on words in PT Sans (643 ms). There was also a significant interaction between font and word frequency, again meaning the advantage of the LexiaD for high-frequency words and the disadvantage — for low-frequency ones.

We did not find an effect of font on comprehension accuracy.

3.2.2 PT Serif/LexiaD

There was no main effect of font on FFD (342 ms in LexiaD and 344 ms in PT Serif), but we found a significant interaction between font and word frequency, meaning the advantage of LexiaD for high-frequency words and no effect — for low-frequency ones.

Effect of font was significant for GD but invertedly: words in LexiaD were fixated at longer (480 ms) than words in PT Serif (454 ms). Also, there was a significant interaction between font and word frequency, meaning no effect for high-frequency words and the disadvantage — for low-frequency ones.

For TVT, readers fixated significantly longer on words in PT Serif (679 ms) than on words in LexiaD (620 ms). Also, there was a significant interaction between font and word length, meaning the advantage of the LexiaD for short and medium-length words and the disadvantage — for long words.

Here again, we did not find an effect of font on comprehension accuracy.

3.3 Other noteworthy effects

In almost all fixation measures (except FFD in PT Serif/LexiaD) dyslexic people showed salient disadvantage compared to normal reading children (PT Sans/LexiaD — FFD: 399 ms vs. 293 ms, GD: 755 ms vs. 368 ms., TVT: 884 ms vs. 497 ms; PT Serif/LexiaD: FFD: 391 ms vs. 291 ms, GD: 546 ms vs. 397 ms., TVT: 771 ms vs. 546 ms). However, there was no effect of the group on comprehension accuracy: dyslexics answered questions roughly as well as children without dyslexia (PT Sans/LexiaD — 88% vs. 94%, PT Serif/LexiaD — 92% vs. 92%,). This means that such children just need more time to succeed in reading tasks.

Besides, we received benchmark effects of frequency and length that let us reassure that our data sets are valid: readers fixated longer on low-frequency (in FFD, GD and TVT) and long words (in GD and TVT) independent of the font. See the same results for adults (Laurinavichyute et al., 2019) and for second-grade children (Korneev et al., 2018) without reading problems.

4. Discussion

Results of FFD and TVT showed that LexiaD is more readable than PT Sans and PT Serif. But this effect is weaker or absent for low-frequency or long words.

FFD results show that if a word is familiar to a reader, then LexiaD helps to quickly extract visual information at hand, for it outperformed the other two fonts. However, if a word is low-frequent, then PT Serif facilitates recognition, whereas PT Sans slows it down (with LexiaD in between). The disadvantage of LexiaD for low-frequency words compared to PT Serif could be due to unfamiliarity with this font. Therefore, LexiaD and PT Serif are better than PT Sans for feature extraction for both dyslexic and non-dyslexic children. To understand which of two remaining fonts is more effective, we have to conduct a replication experiment with adolescents or adults with or without reading impairments. In that case, it will be possible to increase the number of sentences to read, so that participants will have a chance to get used to some non-typical forms of LexiaD letters. Besides, oculomotor control of those groups is more accurate, meaning that they tend to fixate on the center of a word where more features are available.

We suggest that the effect found for TVT is related to text integration stage. Specifically, LexiaD helps to recover from comprehension failure quicker and to integrate a word in the mental representation of the text faster (as TVT includes fixations that not only occur during the first encounter of a word but also after rereading). For long words the effect is absent, but this time it happens with PT Sans. This presumably means that sans serif fonts at hand are more effective for thoughtful reading or reading more difficult texts for any readers. Likewise, the disadvantage of LexiaD for long words could be due to unfamiliarity with this font.

As for the GD, the experiment revealed that LexiaD is clearly worse than PT Sans and PT Serif fonts. Gaze duration is typically considered the best measure of processing time for a word (Rayner et al., 2003) and assumed to reflect lexical access — orthographic, phonological and semantic processing of a word. Apparently, for these stages of word processing fonts with more familiar letter shapes are more effective, as it is easy to convert graphemes to phonemes. To test this assumption, it is necessary to recruit dyslexics with different causes of its occurrence. LexiaD should work even worse if the main cause of dyslexia is phonological processing, but if primary deficiency is due to poor visual processing, LexiaD should outperform other fonts even in gaze duration.

To get an idea on the number of words and/or participants to be included in the new experiments, we conducted the power analysis for the font effect using powerSim and powerCurve functions from the library simr in R (Green & MacLeod, 2016). The number of simulations was equal to 200. The output is presented in Table 5.

PT Sans / LexiaD				
Measures [ms]	*Simulation parameters and estimates*			
	diff	power [%]	N-part	N-words
FFD	23	92	24	128
GD	41	75.5	28	178
TVT	33	51.5	45	296
PT Serif / LexiaD				
Measures [ms]	*Simulation parameters and estimates*			
	diff	power [%]	N-part	N-words
FFD	2	22.0	>112 (31%)[a]	>296 (24%)[a]
GD	26	67.5	76	233
TVT	59	86.5	49	100

Table 5: Power analyses simulations results

Note. *Diff* – absolute observed difference between fonts; *N-part* – the number of participants that should be included in the future experiments to keep the power above the 80% threshold (while the number of words is the same as in the present experiment); *N-words*[2] – the number of words that should be included in the future experiments to keep the power above the 80% threshold (while the number of participants is the same as in the present experiment). [a]More than 112 subjects or 296 words are needed to reach power of 80%. To figure out the exact number more subjects and words are to be explored. However, due to time-consuming procedure max 112 subjects and 296 words were simulated. Numbers in brackets represent max power that was reached when 112 subjects or 296 words were simulated.

5. Conclusion

In conclusion, LexiaD proved to be faster to read in several aspects and could be recommended to use by dyslexics with visual deficiency or those who struggle with text understanding resulting in re-reading.

Finally, we compiled a corpus of eye movements of 3-4 grade children with or without reading difficulties. This corpus let us not only evaluate the readability of the developed font but also explore the influence of linguistic features like length and frequency on eye movements (see 3.3 Other noteworthy effects). This resource can also be used for investigating higher linguistic levels, for instance, whether auxiliary parts of speech cause difficulties in reading among dyslexic and non-dyslexic children. The corpus is available at https://osf.io/fjs5a.

6. Acknowledgements

The authors gratefully acknowledge help in (a) testing and recruiting dyslexic children in Moscow provided by Svetlana Dorofeeva, Center for Language and Brain, HSE Moscow; (b) selection of dyslexic children in St. Petersburg provided by the psychologist and speech therapists of the speech remediation school №3, St. Petersburg; (c) selection of children with no reading impairments in St. Petersburg, provided by the psychologist of public school №491, St. Petersburg.

This study is funded by Presidential grant for young scientists №MK-1373.2020.6.

7. References

Akhutina T. V., Korneev A. A., Matveeva E. Yu., Romanova A. A., Agris A. R., Polonskaya N. N., Pylaeva N. M., Voronova M. N., Maksimenko M. Yu., Yablokova L. V., Melikyan Z. A., Kuzeva O. V. (2016). Neuropsychological screening methods for children 6-9 years old [Metody nejropsihologicheskogo obsledovaniya detej 6–9 let]. M.: V. Sekachev.

Alexeeva, S. V., Dobrego, A. S., Konina, A. A., & Chernova, D. A. (2019). On Cyrillic Letters Recognition Mechanisms in Reading: The Role of Font Type. [K voprosu raspoznavaniya kirillicheskih bukv pri chtenii]. Tomsk State University Bulletin, (438).

Alexeeva, S., & Konina, A. (2016). Crowded and uncrowded perception of Cyrillic letters in parafoveal vision: confusion matrices based on error rates. Perception, 45(2 (suppl)), pp. 224-225.

Castles, A., MT McLean, G., & McArthur, G. (2010). Dyslexia (neuropsychological). Wiley Interdisciplinary Reviews: Cognitive Science, 1(3), pp. 426–432.

Evett, L., & Brown, D. (2005). Text formats and web design for visually impaired and dyslexic readers—Clear Text for All. Interacting with Computers, 17(4), pp. 453–472.

Farar, P. (2011) Introducting the PT Sans and PT Serif typefaces. TUGboat, Volume 32, No. 1.

Green, P., & MacLeod, C. J. (2016). SIMR: an R package for power analysis of generalized linear mixed models by simulation. Methods in Ecology and Evolution, 7(4), pp. 493–498.

Korneev, A.A., Matveeva E. Yu., Akhutina T.V. (2018). What we can learn about the development of reading process basing on eye-tracking movements? Human Physiology, 44(2), pp. 75–83.

Kornev, A. N. (2003). Reading and writing disorders of children [Narusheniya chteniya i pis'ma u detej]. SPb.: Rech.

Kuster, S. M., van Weerdenburg, M., Gompel, M., & Bosman, A. M. (2017). Dyslexie font does not benefit

[2] Except for the first and the last words in stimuli, and skipped words, that are not usually included in the analysis.

reading in children with or without dyslexia. Annals of Dyslexia, pp. 1–18.
Laurinavichyute, A. K., Sekerina, I. A., Alexeeva, S., Bagdasaryan, K., & Kliegl, R. (2019). Russian Sentence Corpus: Benchmark measures of eye movements in reading in Russian. Behavior Research Methods, 51(3), pp. 1161-1178.
Lidwell, W., Holden, K., & Butler, J. (2010). Universal principles of design revised and updated: 125 ways to enhance usability, influence perception, increase appeal, make better design decisions, and teach through design. Rockport Pub.
Liversedge, S., Gilchrist, I., & Everling, S. (Eds.). (2011). The Oxford handbook of eye movements. Oxford University Press. P. 775
Lockley, S. (2002). Dyslexia and higher education: Accessibility issues. The Higher Education Academy, pp. 2–5.
Mueller, S. T., & Weidemann, C. T. (2012). Alphabetic letter identification: Effects of perceivability, similarity, and bias. Acta Psychologica, 139(1), pp. 19–37.
Nuthmann, A., Engbert, R., & Kliegl, R. (2005). Mislocated fixations during reading and the inverted optimal viewing position effect. Vision research, 45(17), pp. 2201-2217.
O'Brien, B. A., Mansfield, J. S., & Legge, G. E. (2005). The effect of print size on reading speed in dyslexia. Journal of Research in Reading, 28(3), pp. 332–349.
Pavlidis, G. T. (1981). Do eye movements hold the key to dyslexia? Neuropsychologia, 19(1), pp. 57–64.
Perea, M. (2013). Why does the APA recommend the use of serif fonts? Psicothema, 25(1).
Ramus, F., Rosen, S., Dakin, S. C., Day, B. L., Castellote, J. M., White, S., & Frith, U. (2003). Theories of developmental dyslexia: Insights from a multiple case study of dyslexic adults. Brain, 126(4), pp. 841–865.
Rayner, K. (1998). Eye Movements in Reading and Information Processing: 20 Years of Research. Psychological Bulletin, 124(3), pp. 372–422.
Rayner, K., Liversedge, S. P., White, S. J., & Vergilino-Perez, D. (2003). Reading disappearing text: Cognitive control of eye movements. Psychological science, 14(4), pp. 385-388.
Rello, L., & Baeza-Yates, R. (2013). Good Fonts for Dyslexia. Proceedings of the 15th International ACM SIGACCESS Conference on Computers and Accessibility, 14:1–14:8.
Stein, J. (2018). What is developmental dyslexia? Brain Sciences, 8(2), 26.
Stein, J., & Walsh, V. (1997). To see but not to read; the magnocellular theory of dyslexia. Trends in Neurosciences, 20(4), pp. 147–152.
Wery, J. J., & Diliberto, J. A. (2017). The effect of a specialized dyslexia font, OpenDyslexic, on reading rate and accuracy. Annals of Dyslexia, 67(2), pp. 114–127.
Wilkins, A. J., Smith, J., Willison, C. K., Beare, T., Boyd, A., Hardy, G., Mell, L., Peach, C., & Harper, S. (2007). Stripes within words affect reading. Perception, 36(12), pp. 1788–1803.
Woods, R. J., Davis, K., & Scharff, L. F. V. (2005). Effects of typeface and font size on legibility for children. Amcrican Journal of Psychological Research, 1(1), pp. 86-102.
Zorzi, M., Barbiero, C., Facoetti, A., Lonciari, I., Carrozzi, M., Montico, M., Bravar, L., George, F., Pech-Georgel, C., & Ziegler, J. C. (2012). Extra-large letter spacing improves reading in dyslexia. Proceedings of the National Academy of Sciences, 109(28), pp. 11455–11459.

8. Language Resource References

Alexeeva S. (2020). LexiaD eye movement corpus. Distributed via https://osf.io/fjs5a/

Workshop on Linguistic and Neurocognitive Resources (LiNCr2020), pages 15–27
Language Resources and Evaluation Conference (LREC 2020), Marseille, 11–16 May 2020

Towards best practices for leveraging human language processing signals for natural language processing

Nora Hollenstein[1], Maria Barrett[2], Lisa Beinborn[3]
[1] ETH Zurich, noraho@ethz.ch
[2] University of Copenhagen, mjb@di.ku.dk
[3] University of Amsterdam, l.m.beinborn@uva.nl

Abstract

NLP models are imperfect and lack intricate capabilities that humans access automatically when processing speech or reading a text. Human language processing data can be leveraged to increase the performance of models and to pursue explanatory research for a better understanding of the differences between human and machine language processing. We review recent studies leveraging different types of cognitive processing signals, namely eye-tracking, M/EEG and fMRI data recorded during language understanding. We discuss the role of cognitive data for machine learning-based NLP methods and identify fundamental challenges for processing pipelines. Finally, we propose practical strategies for using these types of cognitive signals to enhance NLP models.

Keywords: cognitive NLP, neurolinguistic resources, eye-tracking, EEG, MEG, fMRI

1. Introduction

Machine learning methods for natural language processing (NLP) are imperfect and still lack the intricate capabilities that humans access automatically when processing speech or reading a text. For instance, humans are able to resolve coreferences and to perform natural language inference, while machine learning methods are not nearly as good (Wang et al., 2019). Human language processing data can be recorded and used to increase the performance of NLP models and to pursue explanatory research in understanding which "human-like" skills our models are still missing.

Linking brain activity and machine learning can increase our understanding of the contents of brain representations, and consequently in how to use these representations to understand, improve and evaluate machine learning methods for NLP. Our aim in this paper is to find common patterns and approaches that have been implemented successfully when leveraging human language processing signals for NLP. The main objective is to guide researchers when navigating the challenges that are unavoidable when working with cognitive data sources.

In recent years, an increasing number of studies using human language processing for improving and evaluating NLP models have emerged. However, consistent practices in pre-processing, feature extraction, and using the human data in the models have not yet been established. Physiological and neuroimaging data is inherently noisy and may also be subject to idiosyncrasy, which makes it more difficult to effectively apply machine learning algorithms. For example, in eye-tracking, an extended fixation duration indicates more complex cognitive processing, but it is not obvious *which* process is occurring. Brain imaging signals help to better locate cognitive processes in the brain, but it is difficult to disentangle the signal pertinent to the task of interest from the noise related to other cognitive processes which are irrelevant for language processing (e.g., motor control, vision, etc.).

In this paper, we review recent NLP studies leveraging different types of human language processing signals, namely eye-tracking, electroencephalography (EEG), magnetoencephalography (MEG), and functional magnetic resonance imaging (fMRI) recorded during language understanding. We discuss the role of cognitive data for machine learning-based NLP methods and identify fundamental challenges for processing pipelines. Based on this discussion, we propose practical strategies for using these types of cognitive signals to augment NLP models. Finally, we explore the ethical considerations of working with human data in NLP.

2. Cognitive signals

In this section, we introduce eye-tracking, EEG, MEG and fMRI as recording techniques of cognitive signals. We describe the technical details and methodological challenges for each technique and discuss how the signals have been used to improve NLP models.

2.1. Eye-tracking

Eye-tracking signals are recorded with a device that tracks the eye movements in a non-intrusive way, most commonly using infra-red light and a camera. Depending on the sampling rate of the recording device, it provides very fine-grained temporal records of one or both eyes.

When a skilled reader reads, the eyes move rapidly from one word to the next, sequentially fixating through the text. Some words are not fixated at all due to an intricate interplay of preview and predictability effects, and some words are fixated several times due to factors such as syntactic reanalysis. The fact that some words are fixated several times makes it possible to study several stages of linguistic cognitive processing. Early gaze measures capture lexical access and early syntactic processing and are based on the first time a word is fixated. Late measures reflect the late syntactic (re-)processing and general disambiguation. These features occur in words that are fixated more than once. Around 10–15% of the fixations are regressions, where the eye focus jumps back to re-read a part of the text.

NLP task	Earliest reference
Part-of-speech tagging	Barrett et al. (2016a)
Sentiment analysis	Mishra et al. (2017b)
Named entity recognition	Hollenstein & Zhang (2019)
Relation detection	Hollenstein et al. (2019a)
Sarcasm detection	Mishra et al. (2016)
Multiword expressions	Rohanian et al. (2017)
Referential/non-referential *it*	Yaneva et al. (2018)
Coreference resolution	Cheri et al. (2016)
Sentence compression	Klerke et al. (2016)
Predicting misreadings	Bingel et al. (2018)
Predicting native language	Berzak et al. (2017)
Predicting language proficiency	Kunze et al. (2013)
Dependency parsing	Strzyz et al. (2019)
Text summarization	Xu et al. (2009)

Table 1: Overview of NLP tasks where eye movements showed improvements along with the earliest reference.

Each fixation lasts on average around 200 ms, but the variation is large and the duration of each fixation has shown to be reliably linked to many word attributes: syntactic, semantic, and discourse-related. The fixation duration can thus be taken as a proxy for cognitive processing. It is out of the scope of this paper to dig into experimental findings, but Rayner (1998) provides an extensive survey. This psycholinguistic line of research has established a range of eye movement features enabling the study of both early and late cognitive textual processing.

Eye-tracking signals in NLP
Eye movement data has successfully been leveraged to improve a wide range of NLP tasks on several text levels, from part-of-speech tagging (Barrett et al., 2016a) to text summarization (Xu et al., 2009). Table 1 shows an overview of the earliest references for each NLP task.
In NLP, the eye tracking signal can be incorporated into models by using the scanpath which denotes the entire fixation trajectory over a text span. Scanpaths can reveal syntactic re-analysis, text difficulty, and other comprehension problems. Larger-scale computational approaches include Klerke et al. (2018), Von der Malsburg and Vasishth (2011), Wallot et al. (2015). Furthermore, Mishra et al. (2017a) learned the gaze representation in a convolutional neural network directly from the scanpath instead of manually selecting features. This might be a promising approach to increase the amount of gaze data available for training and avoid feature engineering.

Challenges in recording eye tracking signals
While low-cost eye-trackers and webcam-based software (e.g., Papoutsaki et al. (2016)) have recently entered the market, performance evaluations have shown that low cost models have a much higher data loss (Funke et al., 2016). Dalmaijer (2014) and Gibaldi et al. (2017) find accuracy and precision acceptable but they mention the low sampling rate as a constraint for research. Reading research using eye movements are dependent on high sampling rate and good – not just *acceptable* – accuracy and precision. While lower precision can be compensated for with larger font sizes and using only the central part of the screen, it does not seem like the current low-cost models are recommendable for reading research due to these factors. Especially when building a large corpus it is worth considering that any validity or reliability loss such as systematic bias (for example, degrading in precision and accuracy towards the periphery of the screen), as well as unsystematic bias (low data quality due to low sampling rate or large data loss), will propagate to all works using this resource.

2.2. EEG & MEG

The electrical activity of neurons in the brain produces currents spreading through the head. These currents also reach the scalp surface, and the resulting voltage fluctuations on the scalp can be recorded as the electroencephalogram (EEG). The neuronal currents inside the head produce magnetic fields which can be measured above the scalp surface as the magnetoencephalogram (MEG). EEG signals reflect electrical brain activity with millisecond-accurate temporal resolution, but poor spatial resolution. Magnetic fields are less distorted than electric fields by the skull and scalp, which results in a better spatial resolution for MEG.

EEG & MEG signals in NLP
EEG signals have achieved fairly good results for classifying mental tasks (e.g., Zhang et al. (2018)) or text difficulty (Chen et al., 2012). Moreover, Parthasarathy and Busso (2017) presented a multi-task learning architecture for classifying emotions from auditory EEG stimulus. Additionally, Murphy and Poesio (2010) detect semantic categories (i.e. types of nouns, binary classification) from simultaneous EEG and MEG recordings, and found MEG to be more informative for this specific task.
However, there is not much work in higher-level semantic or syntactic NLP tasks with larger number of classes due to the low signal-to-noise ratio. Hollenstein et al. (2019a) achieved only modest improvements when using EEG data for sentiment analysis, relation extraction and named entity recognition. For a review on the use of EEG signals for different classification tasks, including an overview of the ML methods, the artifact pre-processing strategies, and the input features, see Craik et al. (2019).
Further, there has been some work in understanding the parallels between machine and EEG language processing signals. For instance, Hale et al. (2018) showed that neural grammar models are able to learn some of the language processing effects that are manifested in EEG. Moreover, Wehbe et al. (2014b) were the first to align word-by-word MEG activity with embeddings from a recurrent neural language model. Schwartz et al. (2019) use MEG and fMRI to fine-tune a BERT language model (Devlin et al., 2019) and showed that the relationship between language and brain activity learned by BERT during this fine-tuning, transfers across multiple participants and performs well on downstream NLP tasks. In a similar fashion, Toneva and Wehbe (2019) compare and interpret word and sequence embeddings from various recent language models on word-by-word MEG and fMRI recordings.

Challenges in processing EEG & MEG signals

MEG and EEG data contain a large ratio of noise as well as signals from other non-language-related processes, but syntactic and semantic text processing is also known to contribute to the signal. Since EEG merely records signals on the brain surface, it is difficult to draw conclusions about which brain regions are more or less helpful for NLP models. MEG allows to localize the magnetic fields to their sources within the brain with good spatial resolution.

The main challenge lies in cleaning the M/EEG recordings and extracting only the signals containing language processing information. First, artifacts from motor and ocular activities have to be removed. Recently, these tedious manual inspection and cleaning steps have been automatized (e.g., Pedroni et al. (2019)), and efforts to unfold the electrophysiological responses from overlapping, continuous stimuli are being introduced (Ehinger and Dimigen, 2019).

Neuroscientists have studied in detail how to filter the M/EEG data based on certain effects occurring during language understanding, and the activity occurring in certain frequency bands. Two popular ways to analyze the EEG signal are power spectrum analysis and event-related potentials (ERPs).

In power spectrum analyses, the average power of a signal in a specific frequency range is computed. The EEG signal is decomposed into functionally distinct frequency bands. These frequency ranges, which are fixed ranges of wave frequencies and amplitudes over a time scale, are known to correlate with certain cognitive functions. Theta activity (4–8 Hz) reflects cognitive control and working memory (Williams et al., 2019); alpha activity (8–12 Hz) has been related to attentiveness (Klimesch, 2012); beta frequencies (12–30 Hz) affect decisions regarding relevance, for instance, in term relevance tasks for information retrieval (Eugster et al., 2014): and gamma-band activity (30–100 Hz) has been used to detect emotions (Li and Lu, 2009). Hypotheses about the role of the various M/EEG frequency bands in language processing and more general cognitive function are a first step, but more work is needed to establish stronger hypotheses linking language to specific frequencies (Alday, 2019).

Secondly, ERPs are measured brain responses that are the direct result of a specific sensory, cognitive, or motor event. For instance, the N400 component, which peaks $\sim$400ms after the onset of the stimulus, is part of the normal brain response to words and other meaningful stimuli (Kutas and Federmeier, 2000). Brouwer et al. (2017) presented a neuro-computational model based on recurrent neural networks, that successfully simulates the N400 and P600 amplitude in language comprehension. To the best of our knowledge, it has not yet been studied how useful ERP features are for improving natural language understanding tasks.

2.3. FMRI

FMRI is a neuroimaging technique that measures brain activity by the changes in the oxygen level of the blood. This technique relies on the fact that cerebral blood flow and neuronal activation are coupled: When a brain area is in use, blood flow to that area increases.

FMRI produces 3D scans of the brain with high spatial resolution of the signal. For statistical analyses, the brain scan is fragmented into voxels which are cubes of constant size. The signal is interpreted as an activation value for every voxel. The number of voxels varies depending on the precision of the scanner and the size and shape of the participant's brain. The voxel location can be identified with 3-dimensional coordinates, but the signal is commonly processed as a flattened vector which ignores the spatial relationships between the voxels. This rather naive modeling assumption simplifies the signal, but might lead to cognitively and biologically implausible findings.

Most publicly available fMRI datasets have already undergone common statistical filters. These pre-processing steps correct for motion of the participant's head, account for different timing of the scan slices and adjust linear trends in the signal (Wikibooks, 2020). In addition, the scans of the individual brains (which vary in size and shape) need to be aligned with a standardized template to group voxels into brain regions and allow for comparisons across subjects. Researchers using datasets that have been collected and published by another lab should be aware of the effect of these probabilistic corrections. They are necessary to further analyze the signal, but might also systematically add noise to the data and lead to misinterpretations.

FMRI signals in NLP

In their pioneering work, Mitchell et al. (2008) measure the brain signal of nine human participants who are instructed to think about a concept. They average the signal for each of the 60 concepts over multiple trials. Their analysis results indicate that it is possible to distinguish between the correct and a random scan by computationally modeling the relations between concepts. Their dataset has become an evaluation benchmark to compare the cognitive plausibility of different word representation models (Fyshe et al., 2014; Søgaard, 2016; Abnar et al., 2018; Anderson et al., 2017; Bulat et al., 2017). The presentation of individual concepts has the advantage that the signal can be directly linked to the experimental stimulus, but the experimental setup is very artificial compared to authentic language processing scenarios. Recently, fMRI datasets involving more naturalistic language stimuli such as sentences (Pereira et al., 2018) and even full stories (Wehbe et al., 2014a; Brennan, 2016; Huth et al., 2016; Dehghani et al., 2017) have been recorded and facilitate contextualized modeling of language processing.[1]

Besides using fMRI signals to better understand and evaluate the structure of computational models of language, the signal has also been used to directly improve the performance on NLP tasks. Bingel et al. (2016) enrich a model for PoS induction with fMRI signals, Li et al. (2018) perform pronoun resolution, and Vodrahalli et al. (2018) classify movie scene annotations. Recently, Toneva and Wehbe (2019) showed that when the language model BERT (Devlin et al., 2019) is fine-tuned to align with brain recordings, it performs better at syntactic tasks such as

[1] Not all of these datasets are publicly available.

subject-verb agreements. These result indicate a transfer of knowledge from human language processing to NLP tasks. So far, the reported improvements are very small and have not yet been verified on other datasets.

Challenges in processing fMRI signals

As it takes several seconds to complete a full scan of the brain, the measured brain response cannot provide high temporal resolution. In addition, the hemodynamic response to a stimulus can only be measured with a delay of several seconds (Miezin et al., 2000) and it decays slowly. As a consequence, it is not possible to directly align fMRI responses with single words when they are presented as continuous stimuli. The delay can be modeled using hemodynamic response functions or more complex modeling techniques, but they do not work equally well in all areas of the brain (Shain et al., 2019). It has not yet been investigated conclusively whether the fMRI signal is temporally fine-grained enough to detect syntax processing signals in the human brain. Gauthier and Levy (2019) showed experiments where only local grammatical dependencies can be decoded. However, Brennan et al. (2016) showed that for the right features (i.e. a count of tree nodes in a probabilistic context-free grammar model) fMRI is fast enough. More recent NLP studies avoid word-level alignment of fMRI data and analyse longer sequences of words instead (Schwartz et al., 2019; Abnar et al., 2019).

The large number of voxels in the fMRI representation leads to a very high-dimensional signal, but the number of stimuli is usually very small for machine learning standards. In order to fit a model, the dimensionality of the signal needs to be reduced because analysis methods such as correlation or similarity metrics often lead to unintuitive results when applied in high-dimensional spaces (Aggarwal et al., 2001). From a processing perspective, data-driven dimensionality reduction methods on the training set are most attractive because they can work on the raw signal and do not rely on theory-driven assumptions (Kriegeskorte et al., 2006). Examples are classification metrics such as explained variance which capture how much information a voxel contributes to a specific task (as in LaConte et al. (2003) and Michel et al. (2011)). Another option are dimensionality reduction methods such as principal component analysis which reduce the dimensions while retaining most of the variance between responses (Gauthier and Levy, 2019).

Unfortunately, existing fMRI datasets for language processing are not yet large enough to enable direct representation learning, for example using autoencoders (Huang et al., 2017; Rowtula et al., 2018). Instead, the signal is often restricted to voxels that fall within a pre-selected set of regions. These regions are commonly selected in a theory-driven manner based on neurolinguistic studies (Brennan et al., 2016; Wehbe et al., 2014a). Fedorenko et al. (2010) proposed a method to selects regions of interest functionally, i.e. pooling of data from corresponding functional regions across subjects. For instance, Abnar et al. (2019) only include the voxels from the top k regions that are most similar across different subjects given the same stimuli.

Due to the technical requirements, fMRI studies mostly use only a small set of stimuli which makes it hard to evaluate the effect size and the generalizability of the results (Hamilton and Huth, 2018). Minnema and Herbelot (2019) perform experiments with additional data, which also lead to the conclusion that there is simply not enough training data available yet to learn a precise mapping. Furthermore, experimental results are commonly not validated on additional datasets to ensure a more robust evaluation (Beinborn et al., 2019).

3. General challenges

When we want to use cognitive signals to improve our computational models, we are facing multiple modeling decisions. In this section, we discuss the advantages and disadvantages of each recording modality of cognitive signal, the aspects to consider when choosing a dataset, as well as which features can be extracted from the cognitive data, and finally, how they can be included in machine learning models and how these should be evaluated. The decision of which type of signal to work with and which dataset to use depend strongly on the type of research questions that we would like to address. In this section, we provide some guidelines on how to approach these decisions.

3.1. Choosing the type of cognitive signals

An important aspect to take into account when choosing a type of cognitive signal is the linguistic level on which the signals are required: from word level, over phrase and sentence level to discourse level. Due to the low temporal resolution and the hemodynamic lag of fMRI, it is more appropriate to use eye-tracking or EEG of MEG data to extract word-level signals in continuous stimuli. Moreover, if using multiple datasets from the same recording modality, it is crucial to ensure proper pre-processing has been conducted on the datasets, or to apply the same pre-processing steps to all datasets.

Eye-tracking, as an indirect metric of cognitive load during the different stages of reading processing, has numerous advantages. It is an accessible method to record millisecond-accurate eye movements and has successfully been leveraged to improve a wide range of NLP tasks on different text processing levels (see Table 1 for an overview). While the improvements on precision and recall are modest, they are consistent across tasks. The impressive body of psycholinguistic research, a range of established metrics, and the intuitive linking from features to words speak in favour of using eye-tracking for NLP.

EEG is another recording technique with very high temporal resolution (i.e. resulting in multiple samples per second). However, as the electrodes measure electrical activity at the surface of the brain – through the bone – it is difficult to know exactly in which brain region the signal originated. EEG signals have been used frequently for classification in brain-computer-interfaces (e.g., classifying text difficulty for speech recognition (Chen et al., 2012)), but have rarely been used to improve NLP tasks (Hollenstein et al., 2019a). Moreover, there are still many open questions regarding which EEG features are most appropriate, and not much EEG data from naturalistic reading is yet openly available. MEG, however, yields better temporal *and* spatial resolution, which makes is very suitable for NLP. Unfortunately not many MEG datasets from naturalistic studies are currently available.

Finally, the fMRI signal exhibits opposite characteristics. Due to the precise 3D scans, the spatial resolution is very high; but, since it takes a few seconds to produce a scan over the full brain, the temporal resolution is very low. Recently, fMRI data has become popular in NLP to evaluate neural language models (e.g., Schwartz et al. (2019)) and to improve word representations (Toneva and Wehbe, 2019). It is useful to leverage fMRI signals if the localization of cognitive processes plays an important role and to investigate theories about specialized processing areas. Unfortunately fMRI scans are less accessible and more expensive.

Evidently, human language processing recordings are very noisy. Therefore, if possible it is advisable to work with multiple datasets of the same modality, or to work with multiple modalities to achieve more robust results.

It is insightful to run experiments on multiple cognitive datasets of the same modality. This ensures that the NLP models are not merely picking up on the noise in the cognitive data, but actually learning from language processing specific signals. For instance, Hollenstein and Zhang (2019) combine gaze feature from three corpora, and Mensch et al. (2017) learn a shared representation across many fMRI datasets.

Working with data from multiple modalities is also recommendable. For instance, Schwartz et al. (2019) used both MEG and fMRI data to inform language representations, and were able to show how using both modalities simultaneously improves their predictions. Furthermore, Hollenstein et al. (2019b) presented a framework for cognitive word embedding evaluation, where embeddings are evaluated by predicting eye-tracking, EEG and fMRI signals from 15 different datasets. Their results show clear correlations between these three modalities. Barrett et al. (2018b) combined eye-tracking features with prosodic features, keystroke logs from different corpora, and pre-trained word embeddings for part-of-speech induction and chunking. Several methods were used to project the features into a shared feature space and canonical correlation analysis yielded the best results (Faruqui and Dyer, 2014).

Some studies provide data from multiple modalities recorded at different times on different subjects, but on the same stimulus: For example, the UCL corpus (Frank et al., 2013) contains self-paced reading times and eye-tracking data, and was later extended with EEG data (Frank et al., 2015). Similarly, self-paced reading times and fMRI were recorded for the Natural Stories Corpus (Futrell et al., 2018; Shain et al., 2019); EEG and fMRI were recorded for the Alice corpus (Brennan et al., 2016; Hale et al., 2018).

For some sources, data from co-registration studies is available, which means two modalities were recorded simultaneously during the same experiment. This has become more popular, since all three modalities are complementary in terms of temporal and spatial resolution as well as the directness in the measurement of neural activity (Mulert, 2013). Recent reports attest to the feasibility of co-registration studies for studying the neurobiology of natural reading (see Kandylaki and Bornkessel-Schlesewsky (2019) for a review). For example, eye-tracking and EEG recorded concurrently during reading (Dimigen et al., 2011; Henderson et al., 2013; Hollenstein et al., 2018; Hollenstein et al., 2019c) and concurrent eye-tracking and fMRI (Henderson et al., 2015; Henderson et al., 2016). Using data from co-registration studies in NLP allows for comparison on the same language stimuli, on the same population, and on the same language understanding task, where only the recording method differs.

Finally, the presented recording modalities of cognitive signals in this paper are complementary to each other, the information provided by each modality adds to the full picture. Hence, whether co-registration studies are leveraged or simply data from multiple sources and multiple modalities, it is highly recommendable to test all experiments to improve NLP models on more than one dataset and/or modality.

3.2. Selecting a dataset

Datasets of human language processing signals should be chosen based on the research question. It is important to decide whether controlled experiments with clearly distinguishable conditions are required, for instance, if infrequent linguistic phenomena are of interest, or if natural stimuli are favorable to analyze real-world language (Hamilton and Huth, 2018).

As a example for controlled settings, Mitchell et al. (2008) recorded fMRI data from a isolated word stimuli of 60 concrete nouns. In reading studies, serial presentation of words has often been applied, where one word is presented at the time on the screen (e.g., Wehbe et al. (2014a), Frank et al. (2015)). In an EEG dataset provided by Broderick et al. (2018), the participants also read sentences presented word-by-word. Half of the sentences ended with a congruent word and the other half with an incongruent word, so that the difference in the N400 components could be analyzed. This manipulation facilitates the processing and isolation of the cognitive signals, but it does not reflect processes of natural reading, in which the reader has access to full sentences or texts.

Due to the different scopes in experimental research and NLP, it is seldom possible to directly draw conclusions concerning features from these studies to NLP: Speaking in broad terms, psycholinguistic and neurolinguistic studies provide evidence of human cognitive processing of text or speech primarily through controlled experiments. The experiment as well as the textual stimulus are carefully designed in order to isolate a specific cognitive process. Data-driven NLP works towards enabling computers to understand and manipulate naturally-occurring human language through machine learning models based on huge corpora. The phenomena that NLP models aim to model are typically much broader and less well-defined than what is examined in psycholinguistic studies.

Recently, it has become more common to implement naturalistic reading experiments (Hamilton and Huth, 2018). Naturalistic reading denotes self-paced reading of naturally-occurring text without any specific task or reading constraints, such as limiting the preview of the following words. This allows subjects to read at their own speed and results in different reading times between subjects, which calls for more elaborate pre-processing. Naturalistic reading studies diverge from tightly controlled experimental designs and allow the participants to read continuous stimuli, i.e. full sentences or paragraphs spanning multiple lines on the screen. In addition to the more natural setting, a big advantage is the possibility to study linguistic phenomena on different levels (e.g., phonemes, syllables, words, phrases, sentences, discourse), which unfold at different timescales in the same naturalistic stimulus such as a story. Moreover, naturalistic experimental designs, which use language within the rich context of stories, audiobooks, and dialogues, produce results which are more easily generalizable to everyday language use (Kandylaki and Bornkessel-Schlesewsky, 2019). Since generalizability of results is one of the main objectives in experimental science, the potential importance of increased ecological validity in naturalistic experiment paradigms is undeniable.

An example for the use of continuous, naturalistic stimuli is the dataset by Hollenstein et al. (2018). They recorded eye-tracking and EEG signals of participants silently reading full real-world sentences. In Broderick et al. (2018) and Shain et al. (2019) subjects listen to full stories during EEG and fMRI recordings, respectively. In addition to the studies mentioned in this paper, a collection of openly available cognitive datasets useful for NLP in various languages can be found online.[2]

Multilingual neurolinguistics

The majority of research in NLP, as well as most of the available cognitive data sources is in English. However, it is well known that language processing between native and foreign language speakers differs in the active brain regions (Perani et al., 1996). Moreover, second language learners exhibit different reading patterns than native speakers (Dussias, 2010).

Eye-tracking and fMRI studies on bilingualism suggest that, although the same general structures are active for both languages, differences within these general structures are present across languages and across levels of processing (Marian et al., 2003; Dehghani et al., 2017). In an effort to promote eye-tracking research of bilingual reading, Cop et al. (2017) provide an English-Dutch eye-tracking corpus tailored to analyze the bilingual reading process.

Further, there are even differences in the processing of dialects and standard variations, e.g., Lundquist and Vangsnes (2018) for Norwegian dialects and Stocker and Hartmann (2019) for variations of German. Hence, it is not only important to take language-specific aspects into account in the NLP methods, but it is crucial to account for these differences in human language processing. It remains an open questions how many of the referenced studies in this paper would generalize to other languages.

3.3. Extracting features

This section covers different approaches to find the most meaningful features from human language processing recordings.

NLP studies that leverage human gaze signals from reading mostly use a broad range of established features, encompassing both early and late measures of cognitive processing. These features are then used in machine learning systems to learn patterns. Barrett et al. (2016a) use 22 features for part-of-speech induction, Hollenstein and Zhang (2019) use 17 features for named entity recognition, and Strzyz et al. (2019) use 12 features for dependency parsing. Studies that systematically test different combinations of features, generally reveal that using a broad range of established features, such as first, mean and total fixation duration, yield the largest improvements (Barrett et al., 2016a; Yaneva et al., 2018; Hollenstein and Zhang, 2019; Rohanian et al., 2017).

Most studies combine linguistic features with gaze features (e.g., Rohanian et al. (2017) and Yaneva et al. (2018)). Further, Barrett et al. (2016a) use word frequency and word length features in combination with eye-tracking features, because the two properties explain much of the variance in fixation duration (Just and Carpenter, 1980; Levy, 2008). Results by Demberg and Keller (2008) and Lopopolo et al. (2019) showed a relation between regression features and the syntactic structure of sentences: About 40% of regressions land on target words engaged in dependency relations. Moreover, many other properties such as transitional probabilities or age of acquisition could also be used. In Hollenstein and Zhang (2019) and Barrett et al. (2018b), gaze features are combined with pre-trained word embeddings to improve performance.

All these works, however, rely on rather heavy feature engineering. Contrariwise, these features can also be predicted from text: Hahn and Keller (2016) presented an unsupervised neural model of human reading by predicting the fixations within sentences. Similarly, Matthies and Søgaard (2013) predict skipping probabilities across multiple readers. Moreover, Singh et al. (2016) introduced a method where eye movements are learned in order to alleviate the need to get the task data annotated with eye movements. A similar approach is also used by Long et al. (2019). Comparably, fMRI signals have been predicted from language model representations, e.g., Rodrigues et al. (2018) and Abnar et al. (2018).

In general, feature engineering for M/EEG and fMRI data is more a matter of dimensionality reduction. For instance, most studies leveraging M/EEG data for NLP average the signals over all electrodes or sensors (e.g., Wehbe et al. (2014b)). Moreover, methods such as principal component analysis are often used to reduce the dimensions of both M/EEG and fMRI data. In the case of fMRI data, we mention several strategies for voxel selection in Section 2.3. to reduce the number of dimensions. For M/EEG signals, it is also possible to work with frequency band features or ERPs based on neurolinguistic findings (see Section 2.2.). However, these features have not yet been explored in detail to improve NLP tasks.

Aggregating features

Controlled psycholinguistic studies include multiple subjects to obtain significant differences considering the effect

[2]https://github.com/norahollenstein/cognitiveNLP-dataCollection

sizes of interest (Vasishth et al., 2018). In many NLP studies that use eye movements as word representations, eye movement metrics are averaged over several readers arguing for more stability and less noise, but most studies are limited by number of words and readers in the provided corpora (Rohanian et al., 2017; Yaneva et al., 2018; Mishra et al., 2017b; Hollenstein et al., 2019a). But how many subjects are required to obtain a robust average signal for NLP? Gaze annotation can never be a gold annotation, irrespective of the number of readers. It is intrinsically noisy and there is no uniquely correct reading pattern. Skilled readers will exhibit a more idiosyncratic reading behaviour under similar conditions. Language learners or readers with reading impairments will exhibit a noisier signal, that is difficult to use in NLP (Bingel et al., 2018). Takmaz et al. (2019) compared aggregated gaze features and sequential features for generating image captions.

Hollenstein et al. (2019a) used eye movement and EEG features to improve named entity recognition, relation classification and sentiment classification. They showed that averaging over ten skilled native readers is able to diminish the noise and variability between subjects, to the extent where the average worked almost as good as the best individual reader, for both gaze and EEG models. While subject variability is even larger in fMRI signals, averaging over participants can help to avoid overfitting (Bingel et al., 2016). Moreover, Schwartz et al. (2019) showed how a language model fine-tuned with fMRI brain activity data transfers across multiple participants.

Word-level signals

In some studies, averages of gaze features over word types have been used to alleviate the need of having gaze data at test time, and even achieved better results than token-level features (Barrett et al., 2016a; Hollenstein and Zhang, 2019). Klerke and Plank (2019) analyzed this in detail for PoS tagging and found that content words are especially sensitive to type-level gaze features.

For recordings of continuous stimuli, the EEG samples have to be mapped to the points in time where a word (or phrase) was heard or read. Hauk and Pulvermüller (2004) presented evidence that lexical access from written word stimuli is an early process that follows stimulus presentation by less than 200 ms. Between 200-500ms, the word's semantic properties are processed (Wehbe et al., 2014b). Moreover, Dimigen et al. (2011) studied the linguistic effects of eye movements and EEG signal co-registration in natural reading and showed that they accurately represent lexical processing. This suggest that, in the case of reading, the brain processes words when they are fixated for the first time, so that by mapping the EEG samples to the corresponding reading times it is possible to extract word-level EEG features. In combination with the eye-tracking, the high sampling rate of EEG allows us to get a definable signal for each token. In case of listening, the EEG signals can simply be mapped to the timestamps of the utterances. Analogous to the type aggregation approach described for eye-tracking signals, token-level EEG and fMRI features can be aggregated on word type level (Hollenstein et al., 2019a; Bingel et al., 2016). This eliminates the need of recorded data at test time, however the results are more promising for eye-tracking data than for brain activity.

In the case of fMRI, however, extracting token-level or type-level signals from continuous stimuli is less recommendable. A few studies have extracted token-level features from scans of a few seconds of duration. Bingel et al. (2016) computed individual word features for PoS induction by accounting for the hemodynamic delay using a Gaussian sliding window over a certain time window. Hollenstein et al. (2019b) also account for this delay when extraction word-level features, and then average the word features over multiple trials from different contexts. It is difficult to quantify how much of the information of single word processing is captured in these signals. In fMRI studies, models are most often trained separately for each subject due to the large individual differences. It is, however, also possible to learn a shared representation between subjects (Vodrahalli et al., 2018). Additionally, the signal can be averaged if multiple trials are available per stimulus as in Mitchell et al. (2008).

3.4. Including the features in the models

This section describes the most common machine learning methods for leveraging human cognitive processing for NLP. In most applications of systems using human data, it is sub-optimal to require real-time human features at test time. For eye-tracking, there are several studies working towards not requiring recordings during inference. We start by outlining those methods and move to other cognitive signals thereafter.

When using human language processing data recorded from continuous stimuli, it is intuitive to implement sequence labelling or sequence classification approaches. For instance, Strzyz et al. (2019) argue in favor of using bidirectional LSTMs for predicting eye-movement information. Many of other studies have leveraged similar neural architectures, for example, Klerke et al. (2016) and Hollenstein and Zhang (2019).

A basic approach is to include cognitive features as multi-dimensional vectors to represent each word, possibly along with other word-based features. For instace, Rohanian et al. (2017), Barrett and Søgaard (2015) and Yaneva et al. (2018) implemented this approach for eye-tracking data. However, this requires gaze data at test time. Barrett et al. (2016a) and Barrett et al. (2016b) showed that word-type averages of gaze features yielded better results for PoS induction than token-level features. In this case, gaze representations are used similarly to word embeddings, with which they can also be combined (Barrett et al., 2018b). Klerke and Plank (2019) analyzed this in detail for PoS tagging and showed that word type variance was better than individual gaze representations and less aggregated gaze features. Additionally, Hollenstein and Zhang (2019) showed the same advantages of type-level aggregated features for improving named entity recognition on corpora with no available gaze features during training *and* testing. However, type aggregation on EEG data has not shown the same positive benefits (Hollenstein et al., 2019a).

Concatenating cognitive features has also been tested with brain activity data. Bingel et al. (2016) concatenate extracted fMRI vectors from multiple subjects with linguistic features. Moreover, Schwartz et al. (2019) include fMRI and MEG data to augment a language model by fine-tuning a model trained on textual input with brain activity signals. In addition, multi-task learning is a method of training a system that inherently does not need human data on the test set. Multi-task learning studies typically use only one feature, but that is most likely due to constraints in the model architecture, i.e. an increasing number of parameters leading to longer training times. Hollenstein et al. (2019a) trained multi-task learning models to learn eye-tracking and EEG features at the same time as NLP tasks such as sentiment analysis and relation detection. Multi-task learning has also been successful when generalizing across subjects from EEG data, for applications such as brain-computer interfaces (Alamgir et al., 2010). Leveraging eye-tracking data, González-Garduño and Søgaard (2017), Klerke et al. (2016) and Klerke and Plank (2019) employ a multi-task learning setup for text compression, readability prediction, and syntactic tagging, respectively, while also learning to predict a gaze feature as an auxiliary task.

Lastly, another related option is to regularise the attention of a recurrent neural network with human data for sequence classification. Attention weights influence the relative importance of each word on the model, but require large amounts of data to be trained. Barrett et al. (2018a) used sentences from the main dataset to update the model parameters, while sentences from a smaller, non-overlapping eye-tracking corpus were used to only train the attention function. Regularising the attention function could also be done using other human measures such as EEG.

3.5. Measuring improvements

On one hand, natural language understanding models are mostly optimized for performance on specific tasks and typically do not transfer well to other tasks or even other datasets (Talman and Chatzikyriakidis, 2019). On the other hand, cognitive signals are typically constrained to their experimental design and stimuli. These discrepancies may lead to limitations in the possible improvements when leveraging cognitive signals to enhance NLP models.

Indeed, the improvements achieved with cognitive signals are often modest. Therefore, we want to highlight the importance of robust baselines and proper significance testing. Examples of strong baselines are, for instance, word frequency for eye-tracking signals to ensure that the cognitive features add more to the model than purely lexical aspects; or comparing EEG and fMRI feature vectors to random vectors to guarantee that the cognitive features contain more than added dimensions of noise. Additionally, after achieving better results than strong baseline models, one needs to ascertain that the improvements are not due to some artifacts in the cognitive data. Hence, it is vital to perform suitable significance tests, such as permutation tests (Dror et al., 2018).

Furthermore, Gauthier and Ivanova (2018) propose three highly sensible strategies for making language decoding studies from brain activity more interpretable: (1) committing to a specific mechanism and task, which would help to distinctly link brain activity features to specific NLP tasks, (2) dividing the input feature space into subsets that capture representations optimized for a particular task, and (3) explicitly measuring explained variance to evaluate the extent to which each model component explain the overall brain responses.

4. Ethical considerations

To conclude this paper, we address some of the ethical considerations that arise when working with human language processing signals for NLP. As researchers in this area, we mostly make use of existing datasets that have been collected by psychology researchers. Nevertheless, the following ethical aspects should be taken into account.

First, we want to highlight the necessity of considering the high-level consequences of our work. It becomes increasingly relevant to examine the implications of the interaction between humans and machines, between what can be recorded from a human brain and what can be extracted from those signals. What is the potential of the derived results? What is the objective of the final application? What is the impact on people and society? Suster et al. (2017) describe this aspect as the dual use of data: Applications leveraging cognitive cues for improving NLP (and many other machine learning applications) have the potential to be applied in both beneficial and harmful ways.

Second, it is essential to remember the responsibility towards research subjects and towards protecting the individual (Suster et al., 2017). All collected data comes from humans willing to share their brain activity for research. Hence, the participants as well as their data should be treated respectfully, even if as NLP practitioners we are leveraging provided data and not recording it ourselves. Although the data is anonymized after recording, we should refrain from drawing inferences from our models back to single participants.

Finally, the origins of the data and any biases within them should be considered. Most psychological studies are based on Western, educated, industrialized, rich, and democratic research participants (so-called *WEIRD*, Henrich et al. (2010)). By assuming that human nature is so universal that findings on this group would translate to all other demographics, this has led to a heavily biased collection of psychological data. The potential consequences of exclusion or demographic misrepresentation should not be ignored (Hovy and Spruit, 2016). One step further, Caliskan et al. (2017) showed that text corpora contain recoverable and accurate imprints of our historic biases. These biases can be extracted from text, and are also reflected in eye movements and brain activity recordings (Wu et al., 2012; Herlitz and Lovén, 2013; Fabi and Leuthold, 2018). Thus, it is very important to remember that with extensive reuse of the same corpora these biases – participant sampling as well as experimental biases – are propagated to many experiments, and researchers should be careful in the interpretation of the results.

Acknowledgements

Author L. Beinborn was funded by the Netherlands Organisation for Scientific Research, through a Gravitation Grant 024.001.006 to the Language in Interaction Consortium.

Bibliographical References

Abnar, S., Ahmed, R., Mijnheer, M., and Zuidema, W. (2018). Experiential, distributional and dependency-based word embeddings have complementary roles in decoding brain activity. In *Proceedings of the 8th Workshop on Cognitive Modeling and Computational Linguistics (CMCL 2018)*, pages 57–66.

Abnar, S., Beinborn, L., Choenni, R., and Zuidema, W. (2019). Blackbox meets blackbox: Representational similarity & stability analysis of neural language models and brains. In *Proceedings of the 2019 ACL Workshop BlackboxNLP: Analyzing and Interpreting Neural Networks for NLP*, pages 191–203.

Aggarwal, C. C., Hinneburg, A., and Keim, D. A. (2001). On the surprising behavior of distance metrics in high dimensional space. In Jan Van den Bussche et al., editors, *Database Theory — ICDT 2001*, pages 420–434, Berlin, Heidelberg. Springer Berlin Heidelberg.

Alamgir, M., Grosse-Wentrup, M., and Altun, Y. (2010). Multitask learning for brain-computer interfaces. In *Proceedings of the thirteenth international conference on artificial intelligence and statistics*, pages 17–24.

Alday, P. M. (2019). M/EEG analysis of naturalistic stories: a review from speech to language processing. *Language, Cognition and Neuroscience*, 34(4):457–473.

Anderson, A. J., Kiela, D., Clark, S., and Poesio, M. (2017). Visually grounded and textual semantic models differentially decode brain activity associated with concrete and abstract nouns. *Transactions of the Association for Computational Linguistics*, 5:17–30.

Barrett, M. and Søgaard, A. (2015). Reading behavior predicts syntactic categories. In *Proceedings of the nineteenth conference on computational natural language learning*, pages 345–249.

Barrett, M., Bingel, J., Keller, F., and Søgaard, A. (2016a). Weakly supervised part-of-speech tagging using eye-tracking data. In *Proceedings of the 54th Annual Meeting of the Association for Computational Linguistics*, volume 2, pages 579–584.

Barrett, M., Keller, F., and Søgaard, A. (2016b). Cross-lingual transfer of correlations between parts of speech and gaze features. In *Proceedings of the 26th International Conference on Computational Linguistics: Technical Papers*, pages 1330–1339.

Barrett, M., Bingel, J., Hollenstein, N., Rei, M., and Søgaard, A. (2018a). Sequence classification with human attention. In *Proceedings of the 22nd Conference on Computational Natural Language Learning*, pages 302–312.

Barrett, M., González-Garduño, A. V., Frermann, L., and Søgaard, A. (2018b). Unsupervised induction of linguistic categories with records of reading, speaking, and writing. In *Proceedings of the 2018 Conference of the North American Chapter of the Association for Computational Linguistics: Human Language Technologies, Volume 1 (Long Papers)*, pages 2028–2038.

Beinborn, L., Abnar, S., and Choenni, R. (2019). Robust evaluation of language-brain encoding experiments. *arXiv preprint arXiv:1904.02547*.

Berzak, Y., Nakamura, C., Flynn, S., and Katz, B. (2017). Predicting native language from gaze. In *Proceedings of the 55th Annual Meeting of the Association for Computational Linguistics (Volume 1: Long Papers)*, pages 541–551.

Bingel, J., Barrett, M., and Søgaard, A. (2016). Extracting token-level signals of syntactic processing from fMRI - with an application to PoS induction. In *Proceedings of the 54th Annual Meeting of the Association for Computational Linguistics (Volume 1: Long Papers)*, volume 1, pages 747–755. ACL.

Bingel, J., Barrett, M., and Klerke, S. (2018). Predicting misreadings from gaze in children with reading difficulties. In *Proceedings of the thirteenth workshop on innovative use of NLP for building educational applications*, pages 24–34.

Brennan, J. R., Stabler, E. P., Van Wagenen, S. E., Luh, W.-M., and Hale, J. T. (2016). Abstract linguistic structure correlates with temporal activity during naturalistic comprehension. *Brain and Language*, 157:81–94.

Brennan, J. (2016). Naturalistic sentence comprehension in the brain. *Language and Linguistics Compass*, 10(7):299–313.

Broderick, M. P., Anderson, A. J., Di Liberto, G. M., Crosse, M. J., and Lalor, E. C. (2018). Electrophysiological correlates of semantic dissimilarity reflect the comprehension of natural, narrative speech. *Current Biology*, 28(5):803–809.

Brouwer, H., Crocker, M. W., Venhuizen, N. J., and Hoeks, J. C. (2017). A neurocomputational model of the n400 and the p600 in language processing. *Cognitive science*, 41:1318–1352.

Bulat, L., Clark, S., and Shutova, E. (2017). Speaking, seeing, understanding: Correlating semantic models with conceptual representation in the brain. In *Proceedings of the 2017 Conference on Empirical Methods in Natural Language Processing*, pages 1081–1091. Association for Computational Linguistics.

Caliskan, A., Bryson, J. J., and Narayanan, A. (2017). Semantics derived automatically from language corpora contain human-like biases. *Science*, 356(6334):183–186.

Chen, Y.-N., Chang, K.-M., and Mostow, J. (2012). Towards using EEG to improve ASR accuracy. In *Proceedings of the 2012 Conference of the North American Chapter of the Association for Computational Linguistics: Human Language Technologies*, pages 382–385. Association for Computational Linguistics.

Cheri, J., Mishra, A., and Bhattacharyya, P. (2016). Leveraging annotators' gaze behaviour for coreference resolution. In *Proceedings of the 7th Workshop on Cognitive Aspects of Computational Language Learning*, pages 22–26.

Cop, U., Dirix, N., Drieghe, D., and Duyck, W. (2017). Presenting GECO: An eyetracking corpus of monolingual and bilingual sentence reading. *Behavior Research Methods*, 49(2):602–615.

Craik, A., He, Y., and Contreras-Vidal, J. L. (2019). Deep learning for electroencephalogram (EEG) classification tasks: a review. *Journal of neural engineering*, 16(3):031001.

Dalmaijer, E. (2014). Is the low-cost EyeTribe eye tracker any good for research? Technical report, PeerJ PrePrints.

Dehghani, M., Boghrati, R., Man, K., Hoover, J., Gimbel, S. I., Vaswani, A., Zevin, J. D., Immordino-Yang, M. H., Gordon, A. S., Damasio, A., et al. (2017). Decoding the neural representation of story meanings across languages. *Human brain mapping*, 38(12):6096–6106.

Demberg, V. and Keller, F. (2008). Data from eye-tracking corpora as evidence for theories of syntactic processing complexity. *Cognition*, 109(2):193–210.

Devlin, J., Chang, M.-W., Lee, K., and Toutanova, K. (2019). BERT: Pre-training of deep bidirectional transformers for language understanding. In *Proceedings of the 2019 Conference of the North American Chapter of the Association for Computational Linguistics: Human Language Technologies, Volume 1 (Long and Short Papers)*, pages 4171–4186.

Dimigen, O., Sommer, W., Hohlfeld, A., Jacobs, A. M., and Kliegl, R. (2011). Coregistration of eye movements and EEG in natural reading: analyses and review. *Journal of Experimental Psychology: General*, 140(4):552.

Dror, R., Baumer, G., Shlomov, S., and Reichart, R. (2018). The hitchhiker's guide to testing statistical significance in natural language processing. In *Proceedings of the 56th Annual Meeting of the Association for Computational Linguistics (Volume 1: Long Papers)*, pages 1383–1392.

Dussias, P. E. (2010). Uses of eye-tracking data in second language sentence processing research. *Annual Review of Applied Linguistics*, 30:149–166.

Ehinger, B. V. and Dimigen, O. (2019). Unfold: an integrated toolbox for overlap correction, non-linear modeling, and regression-based eeg analysis. *PeerJ*, 7:e7838.

Eugster, M. J., Ruotsalo, T., Spapé, M. M., Kosunen, I., Barral, O., Ravaja, N., Jacucci, G., and Kaski, S. (2014). Predicting term-relevance from brain signals. In *Proceedings of the 37th international ACM SIGIR conference on Research & development in information retrieval*, pages 425–434. ACM.

Fabi, S. and Leuthold, H. (2018). Racial bias in empathy: Do we process dark-and fair-colored hands in pain differently? An EEG study. *Neuropsychologia*, 114:143–157.

Faruqui, M. and Dyer, C. (2014). Improving vector space word representations using multilingual correlation. In *Proceedings of the 14th Conference of the European Chapter of the Association for Computational Linguistics*, pages 462–471.

Fedorenko, E., Hsieh, P.-J., Nieto-Castañón, A., Whitfield-Gabrieli, S., and Kanwisher, N. (2010). New method for fMRI investigations of language: defining ROIs functionally in individual subjects. *Journal of neurophysiology*, 104(2):1177–1194.

Frank, S. L., Monsalve, I. F., Thompson, R. L., and Vigliocco, G. (2013). Reading time data for evaluating broad-coverage models of English sentence processing. *Behavior Research Methods*, 45(4):1182–1190.

Frank, S. L., Otten, L. J., Galli, G., and Vigliocco, G. (2015). The ERP response to the amount of information conveyed by words in sentences. *Brain and language*, 140:1–11.

Funke, G., Greenlee, E., Carter, M., Dukes, A., Brown, R., and Menke, L. (2016). Which eye tracker is right for your research? Performance evaluation of several cost variant eye trackers. In *Proceedings of the Human Factors and Ergonomics Society Annual Meeting*, volume 60, pages 1240–1244. SAGE Publications Sage CA: Los Angeles, CA.

Futrell, R., Gibson, E., Tily, H. J., Blank, I., Vishnevetsky, A., Piantadosi, S., and Fedorenko, E. (2018). The Natural Stories Corpus. In *Proceedings of the Eleventh International Conference on Language Resources and Evaluation (LREC-2018)*.

Fyshe, A., Talukdar, P. P., Murphy, B., and Mitchell, T. M. (2014). Interpretable semantic vectors from a joint model of brain-and text-based meaning. In *Proceedings of the conference. Association for Computational Linguistics. Meeting*, volume 2014, page 489. NIH Public Access.

Gauthier, J. and Ivanova, A. (2018). Does the brain represent words? An evaluation of brain decoding studies of language understanding. *arXiv preprint arXiv:1806.00591*.

Gauthier, J. and Levy, R. (2019). Linking artificial and human neural representations of language. In *Proceedings of the 2019 Conference on Empirical Methods in Natural Language Processing and the 9th International Joint Conference on Natural Language Processing (EMNLP-IJCNLP)*, pages 529–539.

Gibaldi, A., Vanegas, M., Bex, P. J., and Maiello, G. (2017). Evaluation of the Tobii EyeX eye tracking controller and Matlab toolkit for research. *Behavior research methods*, 49(3):923–946.

González-Garduño, A. V. and Søgaard, A. (2017). Using gaze to predict text readability. In *Proceedings of the 12th Workshop on Innovative Use of NLP for Building Educational Applications*, pages 438–443.

Hale, J., Dyer, C., Kuncoro, A., and Brennan, J. R. (2018). Finding syntax in human encephalography with beam search. In *Proceedings of the 56th Annual Meeting of the Association for Computational Linguistics (Volume 1: Long Papers)*, pages 2727–2736.

Hamilton, L. S. and Huth, A. G. (2018). The revolution will not be controlled: Natural stimuli in speech neuroscience. *Language, Cognition and Neuroscience*, pages 1–10.

Hauk, O. and Pulvermüller, F. (2004). Effects of word length and frequency on the human event-related potential. *Clinical Neurophysiology*, 115(5):1090–1103.

Henderson, J. M., Luke, S. G., Schmidt, J., and Richards, J. E. (2013). Co-registration of eye movements and event-related potentials in connected-text paragraph reading. *Frontiers in systems neuroscience*, 7:28.

Henderson, J. M., Choi, W., Luke, S. G., and Desai, R. H. (2015). Neural correlates of fixation duration in natural reading: Evidence from fixation-related fMRI. *Neu-*

roImage, 119:390–397.

Henderson, J. M., Choi, W., Lowder, M. W., and Ferreira, F. (2016). Language structure in the brain: A fixation-related fMRI study of syntactic surprisal in reading. *Neuroimage*, 132:293–300.

Henrich, J., Heine, S. J., and Norenzayan, A. (2010). The weirdest people in the world? *Behavioral and brain sciences*, 33(2-3):61–83.

Herlitz, A. and Lovén, J. (2013). Sex differences and the own-gender bias in face recognition: a meta-analytic review. *Visual Cognition*, 21(9-10):1306–1336.

Hollenstein, N. and Zhang, C. (2019). Entity recognition at first sight: Improving NER with eye movement information. In *Proceedings of the 2018 Conference of the North American Chapter of the Association for Computational Linguistics: Human Language Technologies, Volume 1 (Long Papers)*.

Hollenstein, N., Rotsztejn, J., Troendle, M., Pedroni, A., Zhang, C., and Langer, N. (2018). ZuCo, a simultaneous EEG and eye-tracking resource for natural sentence reading. *Scientific Data*.

Hollenstein, N., Barrett, M., Troendle, M., Bigiolli, F., Langer, N., and Zhang, C. (2019a). Advancing NLP with cognitive language processing signals. In *arXiv preprint arXiv:1904.02682*.

Hollenstein, N., de la Torre, A., Langer, N., and Zhang, C. (2019b). CogniVal: A framework for cognitive word embedding evaluation. In *Proceedings of the 23nd Conference on Computational Natural Language Learning*.

Hollenstein, N., Troendle, M., Zhang, C., and Langer, N. (2019c). Zuco 2.0: A dataset of physiological recordings during natural reading and annotation. *arXiv preprint arXiv:1912.00903*.

Hovy, D. and Spruit, S. L. (2016). The social impact of natural language processing. In *Proceedings of the 54th Annual Meeting of the Association for Computational Linguistics (Volume 2: Short Papers)*, pages 591–598.

Huang, H., Hu, X., Zhao, Y., Makkie, M., Dong, Q., Zhao, S., Guo, L., and Liu, T. (2017). Modeling task fmri data via deep convolutional autoencoder. *IEEE transactions on medical imaging*, 37(7):1551–1561.

Huth, A. G., de Heer, W. A., Griffiths, T. L., Theunissen, F. E., and Gallant, J. L. (2016). Natural speech reveals the semantic maps that tile human cerebral cortex. *Nature*, 532(7600):453–458.

Just, M. A. and Carpenter, P. A. (1980). A theory of reading: From eye fixations to comprehension. *Psychological review*, 87(4):329.

Kandylaki, K. D. and Bornkessel-Schlesewsky, I. (2019). From story comprehension to the neurobiology of language.

Klerke, S. and Plank, B. (2019). At a glance: The impact of gaze aggregation views on syntactic tagging. In *Proceedings of the Beyond Vision and LANguage: inTEgrating Real-world kNowledge (LANTERN)*, pages 51–61.

Klerke, S., Goldberg, Y., and Søgaard, A. (2016). Improving sentence compression by learning to predict gaze. In *Proceedings of the 2016 Conference of the North American Chapter of the Association for Computational Linguistics: Human Language Technologies*, pages 1528–1533.

Klerke, S., Madsen, J. A., Jacobsen, E. J., and Hansen, J. P. (2018). Substantiating reading teachers with scanpaths. In *Proceedings of the 2018 ACM Symposium on Eye Tracking Research & Applications*, pages 1–3.

Klimesch, W. (2012). Alpha-band oscillations, attention, and controlled access to stored information. *Trends in cognitive sciences*, 16(12):606–617.

Kriegeskorte, N., Goebel, R., and Bandettini, P. (2006). Information-based functional brain mapping. *Proceedings of the National Academy of Sciences*, 103(10):3863–3868.

Kunze, K., Kawaichi, H., Yoshimura, K., and Kise, K. (2013). Towards inferring language expertise using eye tracking. In *CHI'13 Extended Abstracts on Human Factors in Computing Systems*, pages 217–222. ACM.

Kutas, M. and Federmeier, K. D. (2000). Electrophysiology reveals semantic memory use in language comprehension. *Trends in cognitive sciences*, 4(12):463–470.

LaConte, S., Anderson, J., Muley, S., Ashe, J., Frutiger, S., Rehm, K., Hansen, L. K., Yacoub, E., Hu, X., Rottenberg, D., et al. (2003). The evaluation of preprocessing choices in single-subject bold fmri using npairs performance metrics. *NeuroImage*, 18(1):10–27.

Levy, R. (2008). Expectation-based syntactic comprehension. *Cognition*, 106(3):1126–1177.

Li, M. and Lu, B.-L. (2009). Emotion classification based on gamma-band EEG. In *Engineering in Medicine and Biology Society, 2009. EMBC 2009. Annual International Conference of the IEEE*, pages 1223–1226. IEEE.

Li, J., Fabre, M., Luh, W.-M., and Hale, J. (2018). The role of syntax during pronoun resolution: Evidence from fMRI. In *Proceedings of the Eight Workshop on Cognitive Aspects of Computational Language Learning and Processing*, pages 56–64.

Long, Y., Xiang, R., Lu, Q., Huang, C.-R., and Li, M. (2019). Improving attention model based on cognition grounded data for sentiment analysis. *IEEE Transactions on Affective Computing*.

Lopopolo, A., Frank, S. L., van den Bosch, A., and Willems, R. (2019). Dependency parsing with your eyes: Dependency structure predicts eye regressions during reading. In *Proceedings of the Workshop on Cognitive Modeling and Computational Linguistics*, pages 77–85.

Lundquist, B. and Vangsnes, Ø. A. (2018). Language separation in bidialectal speakers: Evidence from eye tracking. *Frontiers in psychology*, 9:1394.

Marian, V., Spivey, M., and Hirsch, J. (2003). Shared and separate systems in bilingual language processing: Converging evidence from eyetracking and brain imaging. *Brain and language*, 86(1):70–82.

Matthies, F. and Søgaard, A. (2013). With blinkers on: Robust prediction of eye movements across readers. *Proceedings of the 2013 Conference on empirical methods in natural language processing (EMNLP)*, pages 803–807.

Mensch, A., Mairal, J., Bzdok, D., Thirion, B., and Varoquaux, G. (2017). Learning neural representations of human cognition across many fMRI studies. In *Advances in Neural Information Processing Systems*, pages 5883–5893.

Michel, V., Gramfort, A., Varoquaux, G., Eger, E., and Thirion, B. (2011). Total variation regularization for fmri-based prediction of behavior. *IEEE transactions on medical imaging*, 30(7):1328–1340.

Miezin, F. M., Maccotta, L., Ollinger, J., Petersen, S., and Buckner, R. (2000). Characterizing the hemodynamic response: effects of presentation rate, sampling procedure, and the possibility of ordering brain activity based on relative timing. *Neuroimage*, 11(6):735–759.

Minnema, G. and Herbelot, A. (2019). From brain space to distributional space: the perilous journeys of fMRI decoding. In *Proceedings of the 57th Annual Meeting of the Association for Computational Linguistics: Student Research Workshop*, pages 155–161.

Mishra, A., Kanojia, D., Nagar, S., Dey, K., and Bhattacharyya, P. (2016). Harnessing cognitive features for sarcasm detection. In *Proceedings of the 54th Annual Meeting of the Association for Computational Linguistics (Volume 1: Long Papers)*, pages 1095–1104.

Mishra, A., Dey, K., and Bhattacharyya, P. (2017a). Learning cognitive features from gaze data for sentiment and sarcasm classification using convolutional neural network. In *Proceedings of the 55th Annual Meeting of the Association for Computational Linguistics (Volume 1: Long Papers)*, volume 1, pages 377–387. ACL.

Mishra, A., Kanojia, D., Nagar, S., Dey, K., and Bhattacharyya, P. (2017b). Leveraging cognitive features for sentiment analysis. *Proceedings of The 20th Conference on Computational Natural Language Learning*, pages 156–166.

Mitchell, T. M., Shinkareva, S. V., Carlson, A., Chang, K.-M., Malave, V. L., Mason, R. A., and Just, M. A. (2008). Predicting human brain activity associated with the meanings of nouns. *Science*, 320(5880):1191–1195.

Mulert, C. (2013). Simultaneous EEG and fMRI: towards the characterization of structure and dynamics of brain networks. *Dialogues in clinical neuroscience*, 15(3):381.

Murphy, B. and Poesio, M. (2010). Detecting semantic category in simultaneous EEG/MEG recordings. In *Proceedings of the NAACL HLT 2010 first workshop on computational neurolinguistics*, pages 36–44. Association for Computational Linguistics.

Papoutsaki, A., Sangkloy, P., Laskey, J., Daskalova, N., Huang, J., and Hays, J. (2016). WebGazer: Scalable webcam eye tracking using user interactions. In *Proceedings of the Twenty-Fifth International Joint Conference on Artificial Intelligence-IJCAI 2016*.

Parthasarathy, S. and Busso, C. (2017). Jointly predicting arousal, valence and dominance with multi-task learning. In *Interspeech*, pages 1103–1107.

Pedroni, A., Bahreini, A., and Langer, N. (2019). Automagic: Standardized preprocessing of big EEG data. *NeuroImage*.

Perani, D., Dehaene, S., Grassi, F., Cohen, L., Cappa, S. F., Dupoux, E., Fazio, F., and Mehler, J. (1996). Brain processing of native and foreign languages. *NeuroReport-International Journal for Rapid Communications of Research in Neuroscience*, 7(15):2439–2444.

Pereira, F., Lou, B., Pritchett, B., Ritter, S., Gershman, S. J., Kanwisher, N., Botvinick, M., and Fedorenko, E. (2018). Toward a universal decoder of linguistic meaning from brain activation. *Nature communications*, 9(1):963.

Rayner, K. (1998). Eye movements in reading and information processing: 20 years of research. *Psychological bulletin*, 124(3):372.

Rodrigues, J. A., Branco, R., Silva, J., Saedi, C., and Branco, A. (2018). Predicting brain activation with WordNet embeddings. In *Proceedings of the Eight Workshop on Cognitive Aspects of Computational Language Learning and Processing*, pages 1–5.

Rohanian, O., Taslimipoor, S., Yaneva, V., and Ha, L. A. (2017). Using gaze data to predict multiword expressions. In *Proceedings of the International Conference Recent Advances in Natural Language Processing*, pages 601–609.

Rowtula, V., Oota, S., Gupta, M., and Surampudi, B. R. (2018). A deep autoencoder for near-perfect fMRI encoding. In *Workshop on Modeling and Decision-Making in the Spatiotemporal Domain, 32nd Conference on Neural Information Processing Systems (NeurIPS 2018)*.

Schwartz, D., Toneva, M., and Wehbe, L. (2019). Inducing brain-relevant bias in natural language processing models. In *Advances in Neural Information Processing Systems*, pages 14100–14110.

Shain, C., Blank, I. A., van Schijndel, M., Schuler, W., and Fedorenko, E. (2019). fMRI reveals language-specific predictive coding during naturalistic sentence comprehension. *Neuropsychologia*, page 107307.

Singh, A. D., Mehta, P., Husain, S., and Rajakrishnan, R. (2016). Quantifying sentence complexity based on eye-tracking measures. In *Proceedings of the workshop on computational linguistics for linguistic complexity (cl4lc)*, pages 202–212.

Søgaard, A. (2016). Evaluating word embeddings with fMRI and eye-tracking. In *Proceedings of the 1st Workshop on Evaluating Vector-Space Representations for NLP*, pages 116–121.

Stocker, K. and Hartmann, M. (2019). "Next Wednesday's meeting has been moved forward two days": The time-perspective question is ambiguous in Swiss German, but not in Standard German. *Swiss Journal of Psychology*, 78(1-2):61.

Strzyz, M., Vilares, D., and Gómez-Rodríguez, C. (2019). Towards making a dependency parser see. In *Proceedings of the 2019 Conference on Empirical Methods in Natural Language Processing and the 9th International Joint Conference on Natural Language Processing (EMNLP-IJCNLP)*, pages 1500–1506.

Suster, S., Tulkens, S., and Daelemans, W. (2017). A short review of ethical challenges in clinical natural language processing. In *Proceedings of the First ACL Workshop on Ethics in Natural Language Processing*, pages 80–87.

Takmaz, E., Beinborn, L., Pezzelle, S., and Fernández, R.

(2019). Enhancing image captioning with eye-tracking. In *EurNLP*.

Talman, A. and Chatzikyriakidis, S. (2019). Testing the generalization power of neural network models across NLI benchmarks. In *Proceedings of the 2019 ACL Workshop BlackboxNLP: Analyzing and Interpreting Neural Networks for NLP*, pages 85–94.

Toneva, M. and Wehbe, L. (2019). Interpreting and improving natural-language processing (in machines) with natural language-processing (in the brain). In *Advances in Neural Information Processing Systems*, pages 14928–14938.

Vasishth, S., Mertzen, D., Jäger, L. A., and Gelman, A. (2018). The statistical significance filter leads to overoptimistic expectations of replicability. *Journal of Memory and Language*, 103:151–175.

Vodrahalli, K., Chen, P.-H., Liang, Y., Baldassano, C., Chen, J., Yong, E., Honey, C., Hasson, U., Ramadge, P., Norman, K. A., et al. (2018). Mapping between fMRI responses to movies and their natural language annotations. *Neuroimage*, 180:223–231.

Von der Malsburg, T. and Vasishth, S. (2011). What is the scanpath signature of syntactic reanalysis? *Journal of Memory and Language*, 65(2):109–127.

Wallot, S., O'Brien, B., Coey, C. A., and Kelty-Stephen, D. (2015). Power-law fluctuations in eye movements predict text comprehension during connected text reading. In *CogSci*.

Wang, A., Singh, A., Michael, J., Hill, F., Levy, O., and Bowman, S. (2019). Glue: A multi-task benchmark and analysis platform for natural language understanding. In *7th International Conference on Learning Representations, ICLR 2019*.

Wehbe, L., Murphy, B., Talukdar, P., Fyshe, A., Ramdas, A., and Mitchell, T. (2014a). Simultaneously uncovering the patterns of brain regions involved in different story reading subprocesses. *PloS one*, 9(11):e112575.

Wehbe, L., Vaswani, A., Knight, K., and Mitchell, T. (2014b). Aligning context-based statistical models of language with brain activity during reading. In *Proceedings of the 2014 Conference on Empirical Methods in Natural Language Processing (EMNLP)*, pages 233–243.

Wikibooks. (2020). Neuroimaging data processing — Wikibooks, the free textbook project. [Online; accessed 21-February-2020].

Williams, C. C., Kappen, M., Hassall, C. D., Wright, B., and Krigolson, O. E. (2019). Thinking theta and alpha: Mechanisms of intuitive and analytical reasoning. *NeuroImage*, 189:574–580.

Wu, E. X. W., Laeng, B., and Magnussen, S. (2012). Through the eyes of the own-race bias: Eye-tracking and pupillometry during face recognition. *Social neuroscience*, 7(2):202–216.

Xu, S., Jiang, H., and Lau, F. (2009). User-oriented document summarization through vision-based eye-tracking. In *Proceedings of the 14th international conference on Intelligent user interfaces*, pages 7–16. ACM.

Yaneva, V., Evans, R., Mitkov, R., et al. (2018). Classifying referential and non-referential it using gaze. In *Proceedings of the 2018 Conference on Empirical Methods in Natural Language Processing*, pages 4896–4901.

Zhang, X., Yao, L., Sheng, Q. Z., Kanhere, S. S., Gu, T., and Zhang, D. (2018). Converting your thoughts to texts: Enabling brain typing via deep feature learning of eeg signals. In *2018 IEEE international conference on pervasive computing and communications (PerCom)*, pages 1–10. IEEE.

Workshop on Linguistic and Neurocognitive Resources (LiNCr2020), pages 28–37
Language Resources and Evaluation Conference (LREC 2020), Marseille, 11–16 May 2020

Language Models for Cloze Task Answer Generation in Russian

Anastasia Nikiforova, Sergey Pletenev, Daria Sinitsyna,
Semen Sorokin, Anastasia Lopukhina, Nicholas Howell
National Research University Higher School of Economics
Moscow, Russian Federation

Abstract

Linguistics predictability is the degree of confidence in which language unit (word, part of speech, etc.) will be the next in the sequence. Experiments have shown that the correct prediction simplifies the perception of a language unit and its integration into the context. As a result of an incorrect prediction, language processing slows down. Currently, to get a measure of the language unit predictability, a neurolinguistic experiment known as a cloze task has to be conducted on a large number of participants. Cloze tasks are resource-consuming and are criticized by some researchers as an insufficiently valid measure of predictability. In this paper, we compare different language models that attempt to simulate human respondents' performance on the cloze task. Using a language model to create cloze task simulations would require significantly less time and conduct studies related to linguistic predictability.

1. Introduction

Nowadays language models are the most powerful instrument to transfer knowledge. Mostly pre-trained neural network models are more accurate in any type of task. This tendency in language processing - usage of language model (LM) weights as a part of base model weights - took place after word2vec announcing. Today there are three main ways to use pre-trained LM in different natural language processing tasks:

- Use pre-trained LM as universal embedder for text/sentence
- Fit pre-trained LM on new data (domain adaptation) and also use as an embedder
- Fit pre-trained LM as a part of a more complex and specific model

It is important to note that the resulting system is dependent on the quality of the underlying LM; thus strategies to compare models are also in demand. We propose a new comprehensive way to explore properties of different language models. Comparison of langauge models is not a new topic, and there are many different measures of their quality. Popular modern analyses are the Google analogy task for word2vec (Mikolov et al., 2013) and now GLUE tasks (Wang et al., 2018). However, we want to check the generative ability of several different types of LM and compare them.

One of the key terms in natural language understanding and speech generation is predictability. In cognitive linguistics, it implies a confidence degree of a language unit (word, part of speech, etc.) that can take next place in the sentence (or text). This property of the token in the context is usually measured in terms of the theory of probability, and it also has some well-known probabilistic properties. For example, the sum of the probabilities of all words which can or cannot (in terms of common sense) follow the left context is equal to one. A quarter-century ago these assumptions led to the emergence of the first artificial language models (ALM).

Research papers in the field of cognitive science have shown that correct prediction of the next word while reading a sentence simplifies the perception of a language unit and its integration into the context. Incorrect prediction can lead to a re-analysis of the context which is why language processing is slowed down. However, the types of dependencies between these two facts are still not well studied.

Nowadays, in linguistic and cognitive studies, to obtain data describing the probabilistic distribution of lexical units (for a specific context), artificial language models of various architectures are used or cloze tests are conducted. In a cloze test, participants asked to replace a missing language item in a sentence. The cloze test is frequently criticized for lack of coverage; nevertheless, in terms of common sense, it is cloze test which uses the so-called "human" linguistic mechanisms of speech generation to collect the data. The ALM, in contrast, is basically a set of various mathematical algorithms applied to the text corpus.

Our analysis and gold-standard is a Russian cloze test conducted by Laurinavichyute et al (Laurinavichyute et al., 2018) from an eye-tracking study. We take the results of the cloze task as a proxy for the underlying probability distribution of next-word continuations of partial sentences. The LM based on these answers we will call "human-like". So the uniqueness of the research is that we can compare artificial language models with the model which approximates real human expectations about the next word for a given sequence.

It is important to note that cloze tasks require a major time commitment and are financially expensive. One of the goals of this study is to find out whether the actual human respondents can be replaced by an artificial language model trained on a large corpus, or, whether language models can simulate human performance on this task. Our study compare several language models across four "levels" of prediction: lexical (distribution of surface forms), part-of-speech (distribution of morphological class), and two classes of semantic prediction.

Besides having importance in the field of neuro- and psycholinguistics, cloze task answer generation could also potentially be used for OCR and hand writing recognition, as mentioned in the paper by Kuperberg and Jaeger (Kuperberg and Jaeger, 2016).

2. Related Works

As Kuperberg and Jaeger claim in their "What do we mean by prediction in language comprehension?" (Kuperberg and

Table 1: Example of stimuli sentence from RNC in cloze task with probabilities of the next word. Stimuli: *"А промывать манную крупу перед тем, как варить ее, не пробовали?"* (English translation: *"Have you tried to rinse semolina before boiling it?"*)

Stimulus	Next word	Predictability
А	промывать	1,99E-07
А промывать	манную	9,95E-06
А промывать манную	крупу	0,091529563
А промывать манную крупу	перед	0,000779675
А промывать манную крупу перед	тем	0,015035226
А промывать манную крупу перед тем,	как	0,966154218
А промывать манную крупу перед тем, как	варить	0,011867962
А промывать манную крупу перед тем, как варить	ее	0,04090891
А промывать манную крупу перед тем, как варить ее,	не	0,146951959
А промывать манную крупу перед тем, как варить ее, не	пробовали	0,000829122

Jaeger, 2016), the reaction time is in direct proportion with the predictability of the word: the more predictable the word is the faster is the reaction. Moreover, predictability of a word or a context defines fixation time in eye-movement studies as a result of the language comprehension process. This implies that language comprehension must be predictive. The authors also state that as the previous context expands, the predictability of the next word increases leading to - in cloze tests - higher accuracy of predicting the next word, and - in eye-movement experiments - to shorter fixation duration.

The literature contains several different algorithms for cloze answer generation. In (Zhou et al., 2018) the authors state the importance of next word prediction in language modeling and its potential contribution to OCR and handwriting recognition. The authors enhance existing models with ELMo and BERT language models and train on the CLOTH dataset of cloze tests. BERT models show the highest performance (0.86 and 0.83 accuracy scores on test dataset for BERT Large and BERT Base respectively), as this model was initially trained to recover masked tokens in text. At the same time, the ELMo model's poor performance could be due to the lack of parameter tuning and the fact that ELMo was trained for the next sequence word prediction.

An LSTM-based model for cloze-style machine comprehension is proposed in (Wand et al., 2018). The model consists of document hierarchical structure and dynamic attention mechanism for building the representations between the document and the question. Despite the two-layer LSTM model with attention outperforms one-layer model, the final best accuracy score is still only 0.76 which could be improved by future modifications to the model.

3. Methodology

3.1. Cloze Probabilities

Cloze task described in (Taylor, 1953) is an experiment in which one or more words are removed from a sentence and the participants are asked to fill in the missing content. It is commonly carried out for assessing native speakers of a language, which is aimed to understand respondents' comprehension of a language and their ability to predict missing portions of written texts (Laurinavichyute et al., 2018). This experiment presumes that native speakers can understand context and vocabulary to identify the correct semantic field or part of speech of a missing word.

We used the dataset with cloze task answers from (Laurinavichyute et al., 2018). The dataset is based on 144 sentences randomly selected from the National Corpus of the Russian Language (RNC, ruscorpora.ru) - an online corpus of Russian texts with extensive search options. These sentences were slightly edited: the authors replaced rare infrequent words with more frequent ones and shortened the sentences when they exceeded the preset maximum length of 13 words. The stimuli sentences were subjected to the cloze task experiment. Respondents were asked to successively predict the next words for each context. An example of stimuli that were shown to the participants is presented in Table 1. with corresponding correct next words and calculated predictability scores.

Each context received from 10 to 100 responses, not all of which matched the correct word. The predictability of each next word was computed as the number of correctly predicted words divided by the total number of predicted words. The Laurinavichyute et al. article and the full list of sentences used in the study can be found.

3.2. Corpus-Based Probabilities

For computing corpus-based probabilities, different model types and training corpora were selected. The goal of these combinations is to represent some dependencies (if they exist) between model architecture, vocabulary and to compare results.

In this research, we were solving the task of language modeling - the task of predicting the next word given the corpus. Several models perform well of this task type, including HMM, LSTM, and BERT. We used pre-trained models on our data to predict the next word for each context. These models were trained on different corpora to see how corpora influence model performance.

Hidden Markov Model

Markov chain theory is increasingly used in real-world computing applications as it provides a convenient way to capture pattern dependencies in pattern recognition systems. For this reason, Markov chain theory is suitable for natural lan-

Table 2: Corpus statistics. RNC is the Russian News Corpus, and NCRL is the National Corpus of the Russian Language.

Name	Texts	Size (GB)	Mean length
RNC	470k	2,928	176
NCRL	111k	3,210	2341
(agg)	581k	6138	1258

guage processing (NLP), where data consists of repeating sequences of symbols or words.

In this case, we are using bi- and tri-grams HMM not for PoS-tagging but the prediction of the next word. To eliminate out-of-vocabulary errors in our HMM models, we will use Good-Turing smoothing.

LSTM

A one-layer long short-term memory (LSTM) recurrent neural network model was used (Jozefowicz et al., 2016) to create a list of predictions for each word in the same 144 stimuli sentences. The dimensions of the model are 2048 for the hidden layer and 512 for the input and output layers.

BERT

Bidirectional Encoder Representations from Transformers (BERT) (Devlin et al., 2018) is trained on a masked language modeling objective. Unlike a traditional language modeling objective of predicting the next word in a sequence given the history, masked language modeling predicts a word given its left and right context. Because the model expects context from both directions, it is not obvious how BERT can be used as a traditional language model (i.e. to evaluate the probability of a text sequence) or how to sample from it. We test several ideas: give the model all of the content, except masked word, and using the technique(Wang and Cho, 2019) to rework BERT as a classical language model.

For experiments, we used BERT trained on the Russian Wikipedia corpus (Wikipedia, 2019). To show differences between models, we fine-tuned BERT with our corpora.

3.3. Corpora

The Russian News Corpus (Shavrina and Shapovalova, 2017) includes newspaper articles published in the 2000s. The National Corpus of Russian Language (Apresjan et al., 2006) includes written texts from the middle of the 18th to the middle of the 20th century.

Some corpus statistics are presented in Table 3.3..

All of our models (except LSTM) were trained separately on the two corpora, and on their combination. Thus we examine these models:

- Hidden Markov Models
  - Bigram HMM on RNC
  - Bigram HMM on NCRL
  - Trigram HMM on RNC
  - Trigram HMM on NCRL
- BERT-based models
  - no fine-tuning
  - BERT fine-tuned on RNC
  - BERT fine-tuned on NCRL
  - BERT fine-tuned on both
- custom LSTM model
- hybrid model
  - Bigram HMM on NCRL + BERT fine-tuned on NCRL

The custom LSTM model was trained on a blinded NCRL (excluding the sentences chosen for stimuli) and the RNC. Overall, the training corpus consisted of 577 million tokens. The model was tested on 1000 sentences from the Open-Corpora project (Bocharov et al., 2011) with 1,9 million tokens from newspaper articles, Russian Wikipedia, texts from blogs, fiction, non-fiction, and legal documents.

Among all, there is a Bigram HMM on NCRL + BERT fine-tuned on the NCRL model, which is by structure a combination of a bigram HMM and a BERT model. These models were joined based on the best performance of both models: probability distributions of HMM are used for contexts with length less than 6 tokens, and BERT is used for longer contexts.

Renormalization of probabilities

To evaluate each model's predictions, we took the first 30 most probable words. Each probability was renormalized by dividing originally computed word-wise probability by the sum of probabilities of the first 30 words. This way the sum of probabilities the selected words would equal to 1.

3.4. Overview of Used Metrics

Mean accuracy

The metric is used to compute the mean of correct word prediction across all contexts. Range of values from 0 to 1. It was computed as a mean value of the array of accuracies.

Absolute number of correct word predictions

The metric represents the number of contexts for each prediction of the correct word is non-zero.

Context consistency

The metric represents the proportion of "context consistency". It can be interpreted as the answer to the next question: "How many contexts coincide assuming that prediction of the correct word (for each of them) is not equal to zero for a certain model pair?

Kolmogorov-Smirnov test

In our study, we used the two-sample Kolmogorov-Smirnov test to find out whether two underlying one-dimensional probability distributions of model predictions differ. The null hypothesis of the Kolmogorov-Smirnov test is: both samples of predicted words come from a population with the same probability distribution.

The Kolmogorov–Smirnov statistic is

$$D_{n,m} = \sup_x |F_{1,n}(x) - F_{2,m}(x)|,$$

where $F_{1,n}$ and $F_{2,m}$ are the empirical distribution functions of the first and the second sample respectively, and sup is the supremum function. The null hypothesis is rejected at level α if

$$D_{n,m} > c(\alpha)\sqrt{\frac{n+m}{nm}},$$

where n and m are the sizes of first and second sample respectively, and where c(α) is the inverse of the Kolmorogov distribution at α, which can be calculated as

$$c(\alpha) = \sqrt{-\frac{1}{2}\ln\alpha}.$$

The advantage of the Kolmogorov-Smirnov test is that, unlike the t-test, it can catch the difference between Gaussian distributions with similar means but different variances.
This metric was used to compare both lexical and word class probability distributions of cloze task, LSTM, HMM models pairwise. The results of the metric are listed in the Results section of this article.

Kullback–Leibler Divergence

Cross-entropy loss, or log loss, measures the performance of a classification model whose output is a probability value between 0 and 1. Cross-entropy loss increases as the predicted probability diverge from the actual label. The cross-entropy shows the difference between probability distributions p and q. Kullback and Leibler defined a similar measure now known as KL divergence. This measure quantifies how similar a probability distribution p is to a candidate distribution q. We used KL-divergence to compare several language models.

Cosine Similarity

Cosine similarity was used to measure the closeness of semantic vectors of predicted words between different models. It is widely used for calculating the distance between two words. In our study, cosine similarity was used to find the semantic probability of predicting the word which is semantically close to the target word.

3.5. Part-of-Speech Probabilities

Word class probabilities were computed as follows: each word in the model's vocabulary ($N = 500000$ most frequent words in the training corpus) and each word in the stimuli sentences was tagged for word class and morphological features using PyMorphy2 analyzer (Korobov, 2015) and the predictions of the model were compared to the annotation of the target words. A word class match was coded if the predicted and target word belonged to the same word class. The probability of a word class was computed by summing probabilities of all words in the model's vocabulary which had the morphosyntactic feature in question. For example, to estimate the word class probability in a sentence "A mobile __", where "phone" is the target word, we would sum up probabilities of all nouns in the model's vocabulary. For morphologically ambiguous words (e.g., рот 'mouth' in the nominative or accusative singular), all possible variants were considered in the probability estimation.

3.6. Probabilities for OBJECT-VERB-FUNCTIONAL-MODIFIER

We have also tried to use different tags for our part-of-speech tagging. Instead of using all of the tags, we thought we could use a more generalized set of object, verb, modifier, and functional word, because when a person mentally chooses the next word, they might not think in terms of the usual parts of speech, but choose generally an object, or a description of an object, or a verb, or just some functional word.
Firstly, we converted all of the modified Pymorphy tags into 4 general sets: 'ADJ', 'ADVB', 'NUMR' were generalized to 'MOD'; 'INFN' and 'PRED' - to 'VERB'; 'NPRO' to 'NOUN' (Object); 'PREP', 'PRCL', 'CONJ' and 'INTJ' to 'FUNC' for each context. Then, we have counted probabilities of these tags in the same manner as the usual parts of speech.
We noticed that the generalized probabilities were overall higher than with modified Pymorphy tags - further we will refer to it as OMVF (object-modifier-verb-functional).

3.7. Semantic Comparison

After lots of trial and error, it was decided to use semantic vectors for the comparison of cloze task results with other models in the semantic aspect. All words were mapped into a vector space of the model pre-trained on Wikipedia texts (Arefyev et al., 2015). The comparison itself needed to be dynamic because for each context a different amount of words should have been chosen.
To compare semantic vectors for each context, firstly, we cleared all of the words so there would be no digits, meaningless letters and punctuation. Then, we have built a function, which:

1) Extracts first 10 words (we have decided that that is the maximum amount of words for each context that would have meaningful probabilities as all of the words after the first ten for each model have their probabilities tends to zero) for each of 1219 contexts;
2) Computes the mean probability of remaining words;
3) Counts the difference between the probabilities of the first and last word and then the difference between mean probabilities of the previous word and the next one;
4) Decides what amount of words vectors to use for each context based on how different the first-last word difference and the mean probability difference is – if the latter is lesser than the former, the function checks the next difference, if not – the previous amount of words would be used for semantic comparison.

After the decision on the number of words was made, with the help of `gensim` in Python a vector for each word was extracted.
Then, MiniBatchKmeans (a modified version of the K-means algorithm, that uses mini-batches to reduce computation time, while at the same time trying to optimize the same goal function (Béjar, 2010)) algorithm in sklearn was used to find "cluster centers", or mean semantic vector for one model for each context. And at last, we computed cosine similarity (also with sklearn library) for each pair of semantic vectors for each pair of models.

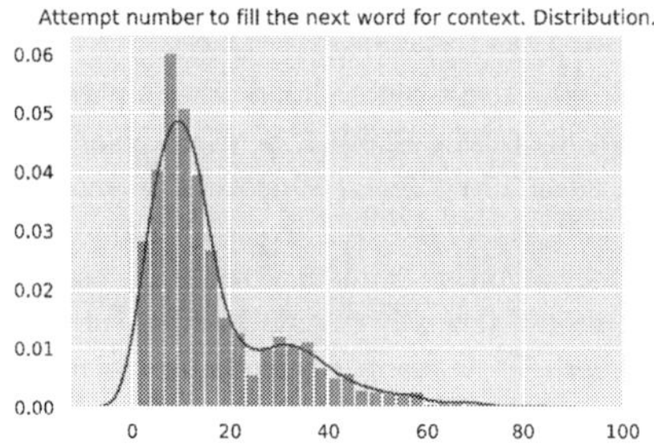

4. Results

4.1. Quantitative and Qualitative Analysis of Cloze Task Language Model

First of all, it is necessary to establish how many different answers on average are available for each context in a language model based on a cloze task, since it is necessary to determine how many of the most likely words will be explored in artificial language models and test the hypothesis about the dependence of predictability on the length of the context.

The mean quantity of predictions for the language model built on cloze-task results is 17 words.

In Table 4.1., contexts with minimum variance in filling are listed. It is worth emphasizing that in all these cases there was no variance in respondents' answers, i.e. all respondents gave the same one answer for these contexts. What is more, this predicted word was the original word from the corpus.

We classified these contexts based on their constraining ability:

- Semantically constraining contexts (contexts #3, 4, 6, 8)
- Syntactically constraining contexts (context #1)
- Idiomatically constraining contexts (contexts #2, 5, 7, 9, 10)

The maximum number of different answers were received for the "на болотах" ("On the Swamps") context - 87 words, which is explained by the absence of any limiting semantic properties of the context.

In this regard, the study of the artificial language model distribution is meaningless, as it will always be uniform, to say, the indicator for each context in similar histograms will be equal to the size of the vocabulary.

Another important aspect of the study of the linguistic model of the cloze task is the relationship between the length of the context and the probability of predicting (i.e., predictability of) the correct word.

The regression line reflects a high value of predictability for contexts of length both less and more than five lexical units. However, the lack of correlation is worth emphasizing. We received the Pearson correlation coefficient score of 0.323 and Spearman correlation coefficient of 0.363.

According to the results of our experiment, the closest probability distribution of the correct word of all the models was achieved with BERT trained on the literary corpus.

In this case, there is practically no correlation: Pearson correlation score is 0.09, and Spearman correlation is 0.08.

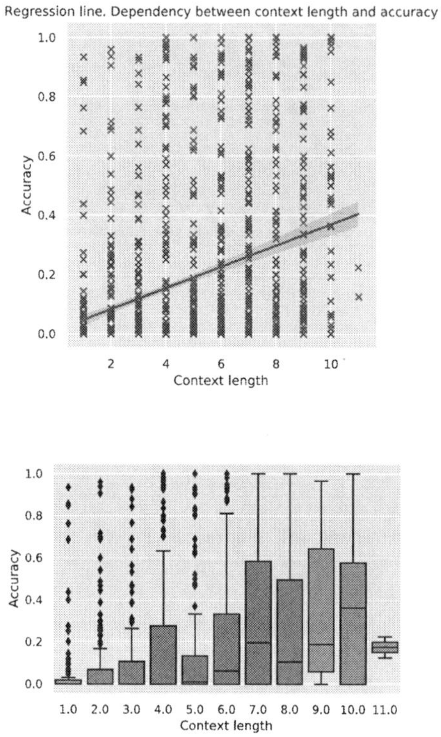

Figure 1: Context length vs. lexical accuracy.

Each model was evaluated by two measures: mean accuracy of model predictions and an absolute number of correct word predictions. For computing mean accuracy, the mean of correct answer probabilities was taken. In case of an absolute number of correct word predictions, a model achieved +1 score if there was at least one correct answer among all predictions.

4.2. Model Comparison on the Lexical Level

Mean Accuracy

Figure 2 below shows a bar chart of the mean accuracy scores of each model on the lexical level. As the goal of our study was to build an algorithm, which would be the closest approximation of the cloze task results (18% accuracy), we can see that BERT (not a language model one) model scored better than the others. Interestingly, all HMM model architectures showed low results on the lexical level.

It is noticeable that BERT mean accuracy results are higher than the cloze task score. This can be explained by the fact that the model was trained on a large number of written texts and thus had a higher chance to guess the correct word. Following this assumption, it is possible to infer respondents' active vocabulary size is lower than the model's vocabulary. Also, we can make a hypothesis that the process of word retrieval by humans and by the model is performed differently, as respondents do not always respond with the most probable answer.

Absolute Accuracy

In terms of the absolute number of predicted words, in the

Table 3: Contexts in which minimum variance is observed in filling by one lexical unit.

1. Какие главные лекарства должны входить (в)
   What are the main drugs that should be included (in)
2. В современном обществе семья и школа оказывают большое (влияние)
   In modern society, family and school have a large (influence)
3. Зачем ему звонить если откликается спокойный женский (голос)
   Why would he call if a calm female (voice) answers
4. Ирине досталась отдельная комната в двухкомнатной (квартире)
   Irina got a separate room in a two-room (apartment)
5. Они не ели целый (день)
   They haven't eaten all (day)
6. Во избежание ожогов надо нанести на лицо небольшое (количество)
   To avoid burns on the face, apply a small (amount)
7. Дрозды и скворцы начали вить семейные гнезда неподалеку друг от (друга)
   Blackbirds and starlings began to twist family nests not far from each (other)
8. Собаку виновницу случившегося приказали сечь хотя в чем была ее (вина)
   The dog responsible for the incident was ordered to be beaten, although it wasn't really her (fault)
9. С нескрываемой едкой иронией отзываются они друг о (друге)
   With undisguised caustic irony, they speak of each (other)
10. Олень бродил среди берез жевал талый (снег)
    The deer wandered among the birches chewing melting (snow)

Figure 2: Mean accuracy histogram, lexical level.

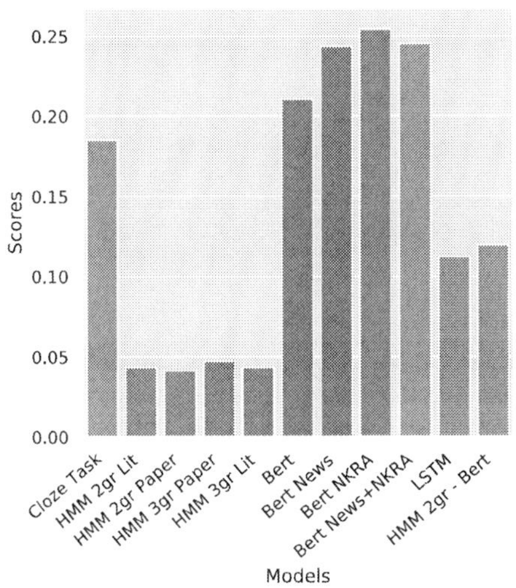

Figure 3: Absolute accuracy histogram, lexical level.

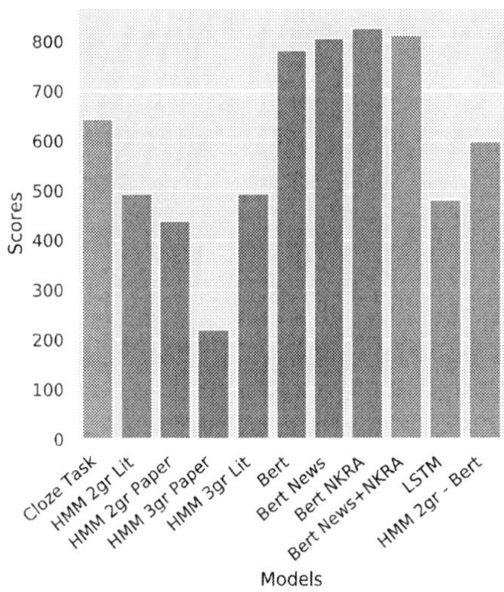

cloze task around 625 contexts were given at least one correct prediction. The closest to that are the results of the bigram HMM model combined with BERT (with around 545 contexts with at least one correct prediction) and raw BERT (with about 725 contexts with at least one correct prediction).

Model Consistency

Next, we compared models' performances using an inclusion-exclusion principle to find the percentage of overlapping answers between different models. The result of this comparison is shown on the heat map below.

The heat map reflects information on pairwise model comparison, however, we are mainly interested in how close the models are to the cloze task model. The comparison showed that the models with the the largest overlap with the cloze task are bigram HMM model combined with BERT (58% of overlap) and BERT trained on RNC.

Kolmogorov-Smirnov Tests

At the next step, we performed Kolmogorov-Smirnov testing to find the similarity in the probability distributions of the model predictions. Figure 5 also reflects the sum value of the pairwise comparison of the contexts using Kolmogorov-Smirnov testing. For convenience, all the values were normalized. Observations show that the closest probability distribution is seen in the LSTM model. However, as we see, there is a variation in metric values from 0.9 to 6.2 for different models. Thus, we can assert that the difference between all models and a cloze task is rather large and in some way unacceptable.

Figure 4: Overlap heatmap, lexical level.

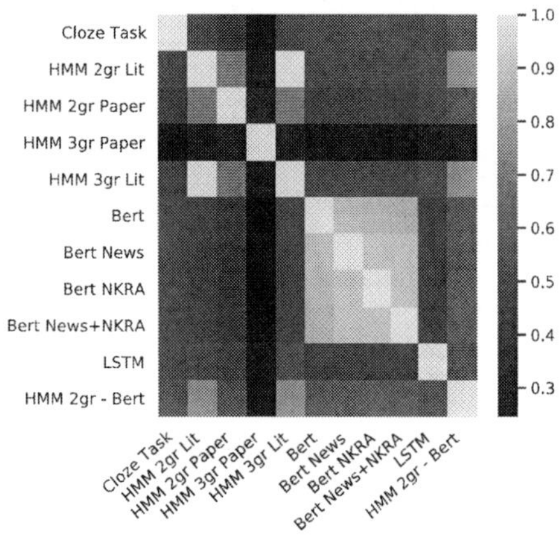

Figure 5: Kolmogorov-Smirnov tests, lexical level.

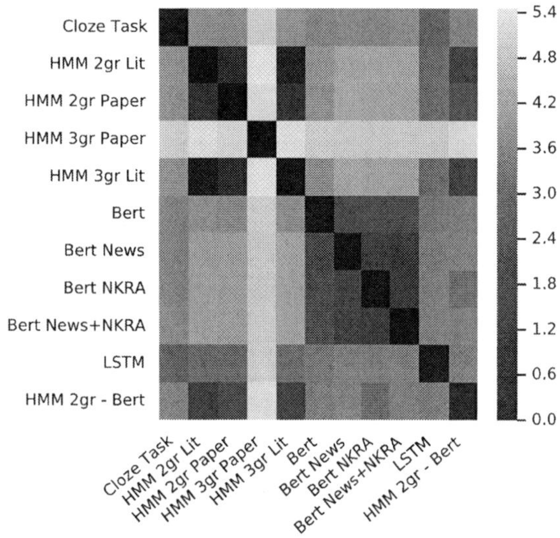

Cosine Similarity

To measure model predictions on the semantic level, the cosine similarity between each context's predicted words centroid vector was found. The number of words was selected dynamically for each context by maximizing vector significance with the minimum words. Figure 6 reflects the results.

Kullback–Leibler Divergence

Due to the fact that all of our models are word-level, and in order to lower the casing variability we've combined all our vocabularies into one. For this compound vocabulary, we calculated the KL divergence of our models.

Table 4.2. shows the scores for three different models with bigram HMM trained on NCRL showing the best results. Unfortunately, this heat map does not show us changes in the language model (LM) distances context-lengthwise. Top 3 lengthwise LM distances from cloze are shown in Table 4.2.. As we see, the bigram models start to increase the distance from 1 to 6 context length, but BERT, on the contrary, starts to lower the distance up to 6 context length. For this case, we merged the bigram model and BERT at length equal to 6.

Figure 6: Cosine Similarity between each pair of models .

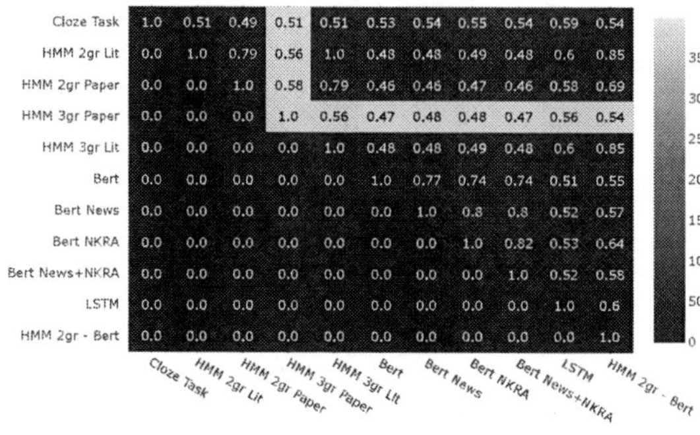

Table 4: KL scores for three different models, all trained on the National Corpus of the Russian Language. "Context provided" is in number of tokens.

Context	Bigram HMM	BERT	LSTM
1	1.34	2.17	2.01
2	1.57	2.10	1.78
3	1.84	2.07	1.84
4	1.79	1.93	1.81
5	1.91	2.02	1.92
6	1.86	1.88	1.87
7	1.99	1.77	1.89
8	1.73	1.69	1.80
9	1.97	1.55	1.63
10	2.46	1.71	1.80
11	2.79	2.68	2.17

4.3. Model Comparison on the PoS Level

Mean Accuracy

The performance of all models, except for LSTM, at the parts of speech level, has significantly and proportionally increased. This is due to a decrease in the set of classes for which classification occurs. At this stage, the first 30 words of each model were tagged for parts of speech. Overall, there were 16 word classes. Notably, BERT linguistic models have the highest scores.

Absolute Accuracy

Table 5: Distance in the KL-metric between the cloze task and language models.

Model	KL-distance to cloze
HMM	1.79
BERT	1.93
LSTM	1.84
HMM + BERT	1.71

Figure 7: Mean accuracy histogram, part-of-speech level.

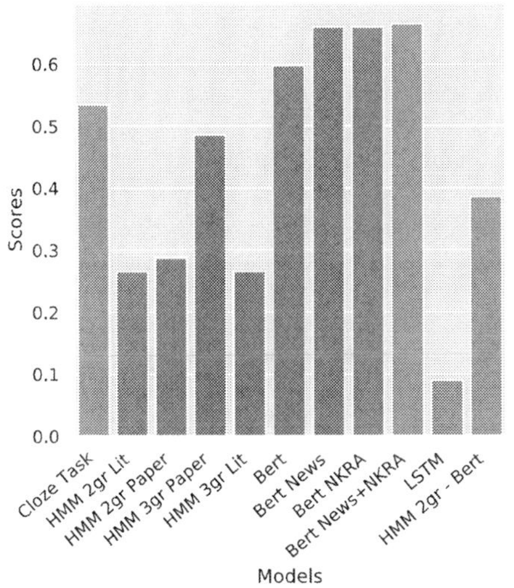

Figure 8: Absolute accuracy histogram, part-of-speech level.

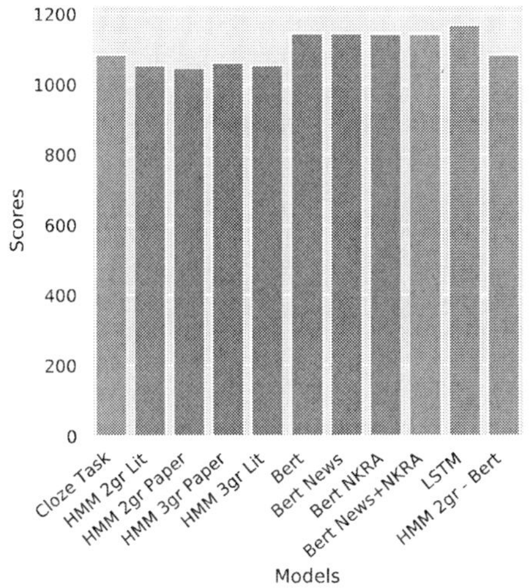

In absolute values, there is also a tendency in higher accuracy of BERT models, which can be interpreted as follows. BERT as a language model correctly predicts a part of the next word, but the words themselves, rather close to the context, have a low probability. Moreover, in many cases, they have almost a uniform distribution equal to 0.033.

Model Consistency

The consistency of a part of speech prediction differs significantly from the lexical level. However, when compared with the cloze task model, we do not see a strong resemblance with one of the artificial models. That is, there are contexts for which a person can predict the part of speech of the next word correctly, while the models are not able to do the same.

4.4. Model comparison on the OMVF level

Mean Accuracy

Figure 9: Overlap heatmap, part-of-speech level.

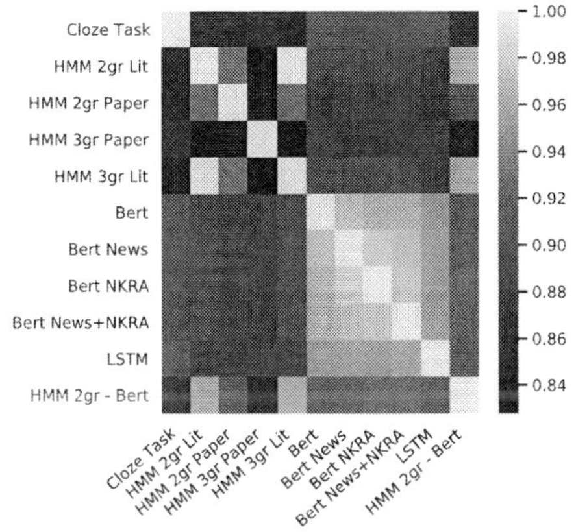

Figure 10: Mean accuracy histogram, object-verb-functional-modifier level.

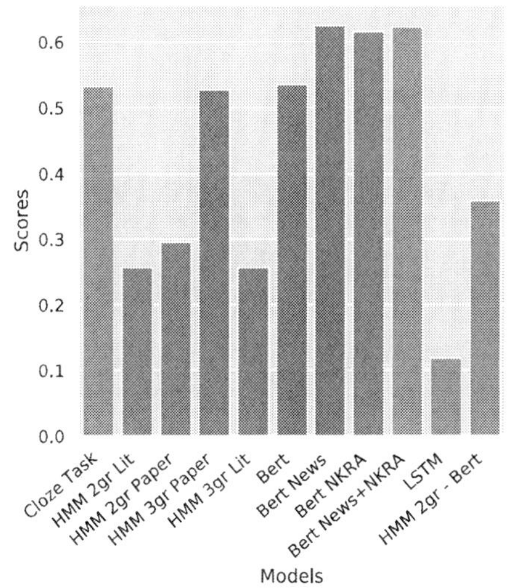

Reducing the number of classes by 4 times does not lead to an improvement in the average accuracy. Although we can see that the models perform similarly as on the original part-of-speech model.

Absolute Accuracy

Absolute values at the OMVF level of generalization cease to reflect any properties of the models. This is due to the metric calculation algorithm. The model's indicator increases by one each time when there is a correct answer and its probability is not equal to 0. Accordingly, the graph reflects that in more than 95% of cases the correct tag is present. It can be noted that for a model with a random tag generator, this threshold would be 25%. Such differences in magnitudes suggest productivity at the OMVF level.

Model Consistency and Kolmogorov-Smirnov Test on OMVF

Consistency at the object-verb-functional-modifier level and Kolmogorov-Smirnov Test are is shown in Figure 4.4. and 4.4. correspondingly.

Figure 11: Absolute accuracy histogram, object-verb-functional-modifier level.

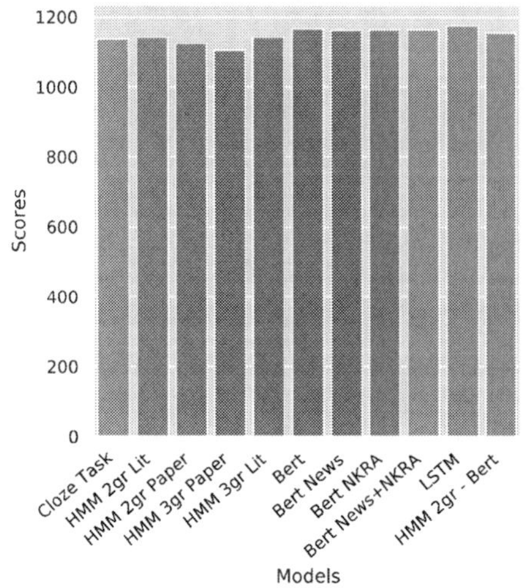

Figure 12: Overlap heatmap, object-verb-functional-modifier level.

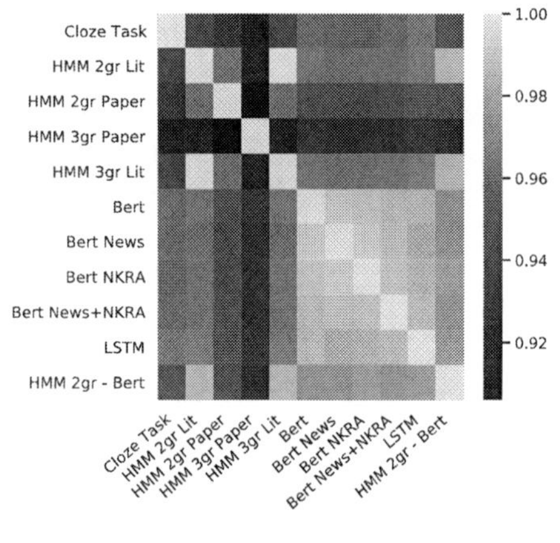

Figure 13: Kolmogorov-Smirnov test heatmap, object-verb-functional-modifier level.

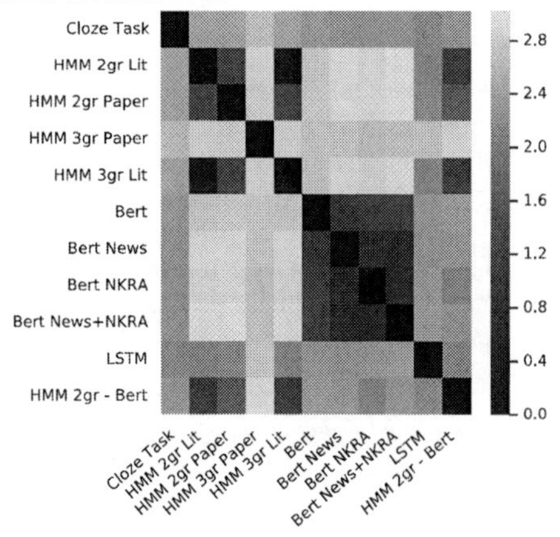

The last two tests reflect a contradictory trend: LSTM shows a greater resemblance to the cloze task. Here it is necessary to comment on probabilistic distribution. Calculation of statistical tests based on probability distributions of the models makes the metrics far from objective, since the variation of the number of lexical units to consider significantly impacts the final output. Thus the results may highly differ for 25 and 30 lexical units. Moreover, artificial models allow us to reflect distributions for the large vocabulary, whereas the vocabulary of the cloze task is very limited and has many random outliers when the context is not constraining the next word on any level. It is disputable whether such cases should be eliminated from the vocabulary during research or not.

5. Conclusion

One of the important results of this study is the development of a certain set of methods (tools) for comparing the generative properties of language models. The starting point is an unrestricted set of contexts and the probabilistic distribution of words for each of them. This data can be obtained from all kinds of language models. Also, the re-normalized value of frequency from the corpus can be used as a language model for these purposes in further research. From our point of view, the most relevant metrics (from presented above) are Mean (Absolute) accuracy is prediction and Cosine similarity measure computed for each pair of models.

We tested this methodology on the following models: Cloze-task-based model, hidden Markov model (with the different n-grams), LSTM and BERT. From the results, we have noticed that the last one can predict the next word more accurately, while LSTM - Cloze task pair shows that semantic directions of k-first words for given context are more similar. However, based on all of these metrics scores, we can conclude that Cloze-task-based model cannot be replaced by any of the artificial language models presented in this paper for eye-tracking experiments. In addition, it is worth noticing that predictability scores computed within the Cloze task reflect the real-world situation, but this is beyond the scope of our study and could potentially be used in a different neurolinguistic experiment.

6. Bibliography

Al-Anzi, F. and Abu Zeina, D. (2017). Statistical markovian data modeling for natural language processing. *International Journal of Data Mining & Knowledge Management Process*, 7(1):25–35.

Apresjan, J., Boguslavsky, I., Iomdin, B., Iomdin, L., Sannikov, A., and Sizov, V. (2006). A syntactically and semantically tagged corpus of russian: State of the art and prospects 1. In *Proceedings of LREC*, pages 1378–1381.

Arefyev, N., Panchenko, A., Lukanin, A., Lesota, O., and Romanov, P. (2015). Evaluating three corpus based semantic similarity systems for russian. In *Компьютерная лингвистика и интеллектуальные технологии: По материалам ежегодно Международной конференции Диалог (Москва, 27 – 30 Мая 2015)*, volume 2, page 116–128. РГГУ Москва.

Bocharov, V., Bichineva, S., Granovsky, D., Ostapuk, N., and Stepanova, M. (2011). Quality assurance tools in the opencorpora project. In *Компьютерная лингвистика и интеллектуальные технологии: По материалам ежегодно Международной конференции Диалог (Бекасово, 25 – 29 Мая 2011)*, pages 101–109. РГГУ Москва.

Béjar, J. (2010). K-means vs mini batch k-means: A comparison. *Universitat Politècnica de Catalunya.*

Chen, S., Beeferman, D., and Rosenfeld, R. (1998). Evaluation metrics for language models. *Carnegie Mellon University*, pages 1–6.

Devlin, J., Chang, M.-W., Lee, K., and Toutanova, K. (2018). BERT: Pre-training of deep birdirectional transformers for language understanding.

Frisson, S., Harvey, D., and Staub, A. (2017). No prediction error cost in reading: Evidence from eye movements. *Journal of Memory and Language*, pages 200–214.

Fu, C., Li, Y., and Zhang, Y. (2019). Atnet: Answering cloze-style questions via intra-attention and inter-attention. In *Pacific-Asia Conference on Knowledge Discovery and Data Mining.*

Halser, E., Stahlberg, V., Tomalin, M., and et al. (2017). A comparison of neural models for word ordering. *ACL Anthology*, pages 208–212.

Hofmann, M., Biemann, C., and Remus, S. (2017). Benchmarking n-grams, topic models and recurrent neural networks by cloze completions, eegs and eye movements. *ResearchGate*, pages 1–17.

Jozefowicz, R., Vinyals, O., Schuster, M., Shazeer, N., and Wu, Y. (2016). Exploring the limits of language modeling.

Korobov, M. (2015). Morphological analyzer and generator for russian and ukrainian languages.

Kuperberg, G. and Jaeger, T. (2016). What do we mean by prediction in language comprehension? *Language, Cognition and Neuroscience*, pages 32–59.

Laurinavichyute, A., Sekerina, I., Alexeeva, S., and et al. (2018). Russian sentence corpus: Benchmark measures of eye movements in reading in russian. *Behavior Research Methods.*

Luke, S. and Christianson, K. (2016). Limits on lexical prediction during reading. *Cognitive Psychology*, pages 22–60.

Mikolov, T., Chen, K., Corrado, G., and Dean, J. (2013). Efficient estimation of word representations in vector space.

Murgue, T. and Higuera, C. (2004). Distances between distributions: Comparing language models. *Structural, Syntactic, and Statistical Pattern Recognition*, pages 269–277.

Shavrina, T. and Shapovalova, O. (2017). To the methodology of corpus construction for machine learning: «taiga» syntax tree corpus and parser. In *Corpus Linguistics.*

Smith, N. and Levy, R. (2011). Cloze but no cigar: The complex relationship between cloze, corpus, and subjective probabilities in language processing. *Cognitive Science Society*, pages 1637–1642.

Staub, A., Grant, M., Astheimer, L., and A., C. (2015). The influence of cloze probability and item constraint on cloze task response time. *Journal of Memory and Language*, pages 1–17.

Taylor, W. (1953). Cloze procedure: A new tool for measuring readability. *Journalism Quarterly*, pages 415–433.

Wand, Shuohang, , and Jiang, J. (2018). An lstm model for cloze-style machine comprehension. In *Computational Linguistics and Intelligent Text Processing: 19th International Conference, CICLing.*

Wang, A. and Cho, K. (2019). Bert has a mouth, and it must speak: Bert as a markov random field language model. *arXiv preprint arXiv:1902.04094.*

Wang, A., Singh, A., Michael, J., Hill, F., Levy, O., and Bowman, S. R. (2018). Glue: A multi-task benchmark and analysis platform for natural language understanding. In *BlackboxNLP@EMNLP.*

Wikipedia. (2019). Russian wikipedia.

Zhou, J., X., J., and Yang, J. B. (2018). Cloze answer generator. *CS 224N Project.*

Workshop on Linguistic and Neurocognitive Resources (LiNCr2020), pages 38–42
Language Resources and Evaluation Conference (LREC 2020), Marseille, 11–16 May 2020

Does History Matter?
Using Narrative Context to Predict the Trajectory of Sentence Sentiment

Liam Watson, Anna Jurek-Loughrey, Barry Devereux, Brian Murphy
School of Electronics, Electrical Engineering and Computer Science
Queen's University Belfast, Northern Ireland
{lwatson11, a.jurek, b.devereux, brian.murphy}@qub.ac.uk

Abstract

While there is a rich literature on the tracking of sentiment and emotion in texts, modelling the emotional trajectory of longer narratives, such as literary texts, poses new challenges. Previous work in the area of sentiment analysis has focused on using information from within a sentence to predict a valence value for that sentence. We propose to explore the influence of previous sentences on the sentiment of a given sentence. In particular, we investigate whether information present in a history of previous sentences can be used to predict a valence value for the following sentence. We explored both linear and non-linear models applied with a range of different feature combinations. We also looked at different context history sizes to determine what range of previous sentence context was the most informative for our models. We establish a linear relationship between sentence context history and the valence value of the current sentence and demonstrate that sentences in closer proximity to the target sentence are more informative. We show that the inclusion of semantic word embeddings further enriches our model predictions.

Keywords: emotion, sentiment, valence, narrative fiction, word embeddings

1. Introduction

The experience of emotion plays a major role in the way people understand and engage with stories. In works of literary fiction, it is the affective trajectory of the story (the emotional journey that the reader is taken on) that propels the plot forward. People read stories because they are emotionally invested in the fates of the characters. In Natural Language Processing (NLP), there is a rich literature on using lexical, semantic and structural information to infer an emotional tag or value for sentences and short passages (Pang et al., 2008; Cambria, 2016; Mohammad, 2016; Liu, 2010). However, modelling the emotional trajectory of narratives poses new challenges – a model must be able to account for both the long distance effects of previous discourse on the reader, and the contextually subtle ways in which the high-level information conveyed by a text can influence the reader's emotional state.

The field of sentiment analysis (i.e. the task of "automatically determining valence, emotions, and other affectual states from text" (Mohammad, 2016)) has begun to answer the question of how we can evaluate the emotional content of text, particularly with regard to commercial domains and social media. For example, work on sentiment analysis has focused on product or movie reviews (Mohammad, 2016; Liu, 2010; Socher et al., 2013; Tai et al., 2015) or on the analysis of twitter feeds (Liu, 2010; Zimbra et al., 2018). Recent work using deep learning, and in particular recurrent neural networks (RNN) such as Long Short-Term Memory (LSTM) networks (Hochreiter and Schmidhuber, 1997), and Transformer networks (Vaswani et al., 2017) has facilitated a significant increase in the performance of sentiment classification of texts and, given the ability of such networks to represent information over long sequences (Socher et al., 2013; Tai et al., 2015; Jiang et al., 2019), they show particular promise for modelling high-level properties of natural discourse, such as literary texts. Most of the work on sentiment analysis makes use of large, readily available corpora of labelled data, which contain short samples of text (e.g. tweets or movie reviews) and associated explicit rating values (e.g. 5-star rating systems for movie and product reviews, or emoticons or hashtags used to summarise or emphasise the emotional content of a tweet (Liu, 2010; Mohammad, 2016; Socher et al., 2013; Tai et al., 2015). However, no large dataset of literary text annotated for emotional content exists, and so in this study we start by developing a method which can learn to predict the emotional content at a particular point in a story given the preceding context and existing word-level resources (such as hand-tailored sentiment dictionaries, and corpus-derived word-embeddings). In particular, in order to determine how the sentiment of the text changes over time we must evaluate the sentiment of each new sentence as it arises within the context of the text that has come before. Our approach conceives the problem of modelling the emotional trajectory of narrative as consisting of two distinct questions:

1. Can the sentiment of a given sentence be determined by a previous history of sentences?
2. How much history should be included to be optimally informative?

We focus on modelling emotional valence at the sentence level. Explicitly, we model the valence of any given sentence in a sequence of sentences making up a narrative using the preceding context. We explore various sizes of sentence history context window and the effects of incorporating semantic information through the inclusion of pretrained word embeddings of various dimensions.

To our knowledge, very little previous work has directly examined the influence of sentence history on the current sentence's valence as we do in this paper. Jockers (2015) takes a simple sum of word valences as representative of sentence valence and then employs a number of different smoothing functions to allow for the effects of history. Whissell (2010) takes a mean of all word valence values as representative of the valence value for different chunks of text (e.g. sentence, paragraph, and chapter-level chunks). In this work, we choose sentence-level sentiment as the best basic unit of measurement for emotional content. We model sentence-level valence using a lexicon of sentiment (Whissell, 2010), where the sentence-level valence is estimated as the mean of the sentence's word valences as found in the lexicon. While we are aware that a sentence valence rating based on a mean of the constituent word ratings taken from a lexicon is not state-of-the-art in sentiment analysis, the approach is validated by work in psychology (Whissell, 2010; Whissell, 2003; Bestgen, 1994) and offers a computationally inexpensive way to begin this exploratory work, in the absence of large labelled datasets.

2. Related work

Most work in the field of sentiment analysis has focused on product reviews, tweets, and emails, and has been focused on determining opinions towards certain targets (e.g. the new iPhone, or President Obama) (Mohammad, 2016; Liu, 2010; Mohammad et al., 2013). Liu (2010) surveys the field of sentiment analysis with a focus on opinion mining — determining users opinions about goods or services by analyzing reviews. Mohammad et al. (2013) trained two SVM classifiers for two different sentiment tasks; the first of these was a message level sentiment prediction task and the second a term-level task. They achieved state-of-the-art performance on both tasks using two lexicons generated from tweets (the first using tweets with sentiment hashtags to generate the lexicon, the second using tweets with emoticons). The use of such lexicons of affect, where each entry is annotated with a valence value, is commonplace in sentiment analysis. As well being automatically generated, as in the tweet lexicons (Mohammad, 2016), lexicons may also be created by human annotation (usually gathered using online tools such as Mechanical Turk).

There are several prominent sentiment lexicons that differ in their contents and methods of compilation. The NRC Emotion Lexicon, known as Emolex (Mohammad and Turney, 2010), is a list of 14,182 English words and their associations with eight basic emotions (anger, fear, anticipation, trust, surprise, sadness, joy, and disgust) and two sentiments (negative and positive). The terms in EmoLex are carefully chosen to include some of the most frequent English nouns, verbs, adjectives, and adverbs. The Opinion Lexicon (Liu et al., 2005) consists of a list of 6800 positive and negative sentiment words. This lexicon only consists of words believed to be associated with either polarity and does not contain any neutral words. AFINN (Nielsen, 2011) is a list of English words rated for valence on a scale of -5 (negative) to +5(positive). The words were manually labeled by Finn Årup Nielsen (the author) in 2009-2011. There are two versions of this lexicon — AFINN-96 (1468 unique words and phrases) and AFINN-111 (the newest version with 2477 words and phrases). There are also lexicons available from studies on emotion in psychology, most notably the Revised Dictionary of Affect in Language (DAL) (Whissell, 2010). Whissell's DAL consists of 8742 English words which have been rated for their activation, evaluation and imagery. Each of these dimensions was rated along a three point scale: (1) Unpleasant, (2) In between, (3) Pleasant; (1) Passive, (2) In between, (3) Active; (1) Hard to imaging, (2) In between, (3) Easy to imagine. It was comprised of frequently occurring words in a number of sources including an established corpus of 1,000,000 words (Francis and Kucera, 1979), samples of writing generated by adolescents, and juvenile literature. When tested against a corpus of 350,000 English words gathered from many different sources, the DAL demonstrated a matching rate of 90%, suggesting that we can expect 9 out of every 10 words in any given English language text to have rating data in DAL (Whissell, 2009).

There is some work to demonstrate that there is a correlation between these lexical affective word ratings and subjective passage ratings (Bestgen, 1994; Whissell, 2003; Hsu et al., 2015). However, these studies have relied on carefully chosen text inputs and have avoided complicating issues such as negation and irony, etc., which are commonplace in natural discourse.

While there have been a few studies into emotion in literary texts (Bestgen, 1994; Mohammad, 2012; Whissell, 2003; Hsu et al., 2015), these have largely focused on detecting discrete emotions (love, anger, fear etc.) and centred almost exclusively on classifying texts (or sections of text) into these discrete groups. Mohammad (2012) compared the polarity and emotional word density (defined as the number of emotion words per X-words) of novels and fairy tales in English. Using the NRC Emotion lexicon, Mohammad and Turney (2010) labelled words in novels and fairy tales with polarity and discreet emotions such as joy, sadness, and so on. They then used an emotion analyser tool to make certain inferences from the data; for example, counting the instances of words related to particular emotions, and comparing the emotional distributions of different words across different genres. However, this work focused on discreet emotions (joy, anger, etc.) using associated emotion words, which can enlighten us in terms of literary criticism or text classification, summarization, etc., but which are not sufficient to help us to effectively model the emotion of a text in a way comparable to how a person experiences it over time as a story unfolds, or how it is constructed in the brain. Reagan et al. (2016) investigated the emotional arcs of narrative fiction using a sliding window of sentences.

What all of the aforementioned approaches have in common is that they consider the task of investigating valence and emotion in literature as a classification problem. The goal is to assign a given text or segment of text with a valence label which can then be used to derive some insight into the author's opinion regarding some product or issue, or to bring some quantitative insight to bear on studies in literary criticism. In this study, in contrast, we aim to model the changing experience of emotion during the course of reading a text. For this reason we frame the problem as a regression task, where we aim to predict a real number (measuring the degree of positive or negative emotion) for each sentence in the sequence of sentences making up the narrative.

3. Methodology

We aim to predict the valence of each sentence using information extracted from the history preceding that sentence. For this purpose, we train machine learning models that assign an emotion value to each sentence given information available in the preceding context. There are three key challenges that need to be addressed. First, identifying the features of the preceding context that are relevant to this sentence-by-sentence valence assignment task. Second, identifying what size of context history is most informative. And third, determining the type of machine learning model which performs best in predicting these sentence valences. As a first step, we investigate the degree to which the relationship between current sentence valence and sentence context history information can be modelled using linear methods. We apply two models to this task — linear regression and a linear support vector regressor. In the second part of the study, we investigate whether the application of non-linear methods to the same feature sets can better model the relationship between the sentence context history and the current sentence valence. We implement these non-linear models using a random forest regressor.

To train these models we explore a number of different feature combinations, to determine which kinds of information are most important for predicting sentence-level valence. We explore the scope of context relevant to inferring sentence valence, investigating different sizes of sentence context history and a variety of feature sets of different dimensionalities. This first stage of our study therefore focuses on the exploration of eighteen different feature sets combined in the following ways: (1) a history of sentence valence scores only (over a number of history window sizes, spanning 10, 50 and 100 sentences), and (2) a history of sentence valence combined with semantic information (i.e. pre-trained semantic word embeddings in the form of 50, 100, 200 and 300 dimension GloVe word embeddings (Pennington et al., 2014), and 300 dimension FastText word embeddings (trained on subword information) (Bojanowski et al., 2017) again over the same number of context history window sizes (10, 50 and 100 sentences). The 18 different feature set combinations investigated correspond to the rows of the results table below (Table 1).

4. Data and Resources

4.1. Text Used

Project Gutenberg (https://www.gutenberg.org/) provides access to thousands of public domain books (copyright expired) in plain-text format. We selected a corpus of 100 books (643,352 sentences) in total. We split these, by book, into 72 training texts (476,891 sentences, 74% of our corpus) and 28 test texts (166461 sentences, 26% of our corpus). The texts were split in this way to preserve the natural boundaries between books. These books were chosen as they represent pieces of literary fiction for children which would be well in common narrative techniques such as the use of irony, metaphors and imagery, and creative language. These are important features of literary language which can prove challenging for sentiment analysis systems based on a simple literal interpretation of sentences.

4.2. Lexicons and lexical embeddings

In training our models, we used information about emotional content derived from Whissell (1989)'s Dictionary of Affect in Language (the Revised DAL) (Whissell, 2010), discussed in Section 2. We generated sentence-by-sentence valence ratings for our target texts using the Whissell lexicon. The valence for each sentence is estimated by averaging over the valence values for the constituent words in the sentence. We then took these sentence-level valence ratings as the target values we hoped to predict.

5. Results

We explored three different machine learning models: Linear Regression, Linear Support Vector Regression and Random Forest Regression. The results from these models (R^2 values for predictions on the test set) are displayed in Table 1 below. We also present two figures which each illustrate different patterns observable from the data. Figure 1 illustrates the difference in performance of each of the machine learning models tested, across each of the different context windows. Figure 2 shows the difference in performance on each feature set across all of the models tested.

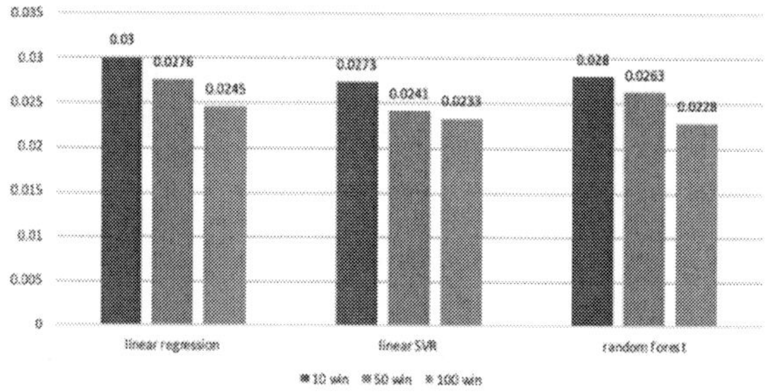

Figure 1: Performance (R^2 values on the test set) of all machine learning models across all context sizes, averaged over all feature sets.

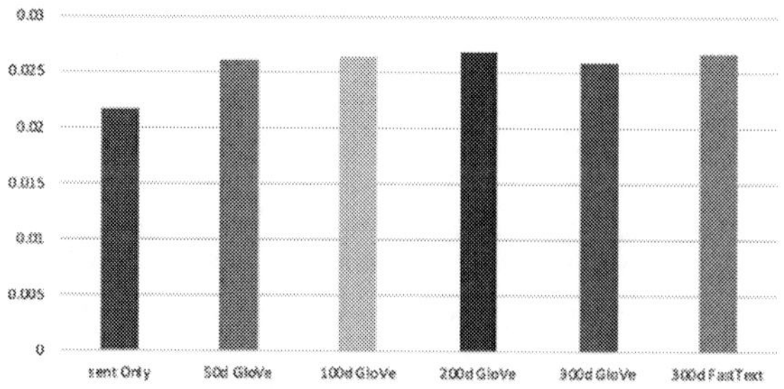

Figure 2: Contribution of each different feature combination to model performance; averaged over all model sets.

Feature Set	Context	Linear Regression	Linear SVR	Random Forest
Sentence Only	10	0.0210	0.0210	0.0236
	50	0.0215	0.0215	0.0226
	100	0.0215	0.0214	0.0213
50d GloVe	10	**0.0309**	**0.0312**	0.0295
	50	0.0304	0.0250	0.0285
	100	0.0280	0.0244	0.0261
100d GloVe	10	0.0309	0.0203	0.0294
	50	0.0302	0.0238	0.0267
	100	0.0274	0.0231	0.0256
200d GloVe	10	0.0302	0.0308	0.0291
	50	0.0288	0.0251	0.0267
	100	0.0259	0.0239	0.0214
300d GloVe	10	0.0288	0.0294	0.0283
	50	0.0273	0.0242	0.0261
	100	0.0235	0.0231	0.0211
300d FastText	10	0.0299	**0.0312**	**0.0310**
	50	0.0273	0.0249	0.0271
	100	0.0241	0.0237	0.0214

Table 1: Performance (R^2 values for predictions on the test set) of all machine learning models across all context sizes.

6. Discussion

Our study has focused on two central questions – firstly, to establish whether linear or non-linear methods are best suited to modelling this type of relationship and, secondly, to determine what kind of features extracted from the historical content are the most effective in training the machine learning models. This second question of finding an optimal feature set can be sub-divided into two smaller problems: (a) assessing whether the inclusion of semantic information in the form of pre-trained word-embeddings adds more relevant information to the model training, and (b) determining if there is an optimal size of sentence history context that should be included to generate the best predictions for each model.

From the results presented in Table 1, we can see that there is a small linear relationship between sentence valence history and the valence of the current sentence. This relationship is statistically significant at $p = 0.0001$. While these results clearly show that we have captured a real linear effect between valence history and current sentence valence, the magnitude of explained variance is small. The application of non-linear methods does not improve performance. However, we can discern an important pattern in these results regarding the influence of sentence history context on our model predictions. We can see from Table 1 that across all models and feature sets, the best results are generated using a sentence history context of 10 sentences, which confirms our intuition that sentences closer to the sentence being predicted should bear more on its valence value than sentences further back in the history. This information is summarised in Figure 1 where we have taken an average across all feature sets for each model to illustrate this trend.

Figure 2 depicts a summarisation of the relative contribution of each of the feature sets averaged across all of the models implemented and all of the context history sizes employed. We can see from this illustration that while all of the feature sets ultimately result in models which exhibit similar performance, in general, the inclusion of the semantic word embeddings does add slightly to the predictive power of the models.

7. Conclusions and Future Work

In this paper we proposed to investigate whether information present in a history of previous sentences can be used to predict a valence value for the following sentence in context. We explored both linear and non-linear methods and a range of different feature combinations. We also looked at different context history sizes to determine what range of previous sentences was most informative for our models. In conclusion, we have established a linear relationship between sentence context history and the valence value of the current sentence. We have demonstrated that the sentences in closer proximity to the target sentence are more informative. We have also shown that the inclusion of semantic word embeddings does seem to enrich our model predictions. We have therefore established a firm base for further explorations of valence in literature which should be characterised by further investigations of potentially optimally informative feature sets and the application of models capable of better capturing the complex, non-linearities inherent in literary text, such as LSTM artificial neural networks.

8. Bibliographical References

Bestgen, Y. (1994). Can emotional valence in stories be determined from words? *Cognition & Emotion*, 8(1):21–36.

Bojanowski, P., Grave, E., Joulin, A., and Mikolov, T. (2017). Enriching word vectors with subword information. *Transactions of the Association for Computational Linguistics*, 5:135–146.

Cambria, E. (2016). Affective computing and sentiment analysis. *IEEE Intelligent Systems*, 31(2):102–107.

Francis, W. N. and Kucera, H. (1979). *Brown Corpus Manual: Manual of Information to accompany A Standard Corpus of Present-Day Edited American English, for use with Digital Computers*. Department of Linguistics, Brown University, Providence, USA.

Hochreiter, S. and Schmidhuber, J. (1997). Long short-term memory. *Neural computation*, 9(8):1735–1780.

Hsu, C.-T., Jacobs, A. M., Citron, F. M., and Conrad, M. (2015). The emotion potential of words and passages in reading harry potter–an fmri study. *Brain and language*, 142:96–114.

Jiang, M., Wu, J., Shi, X., and Zhang, M. (2019). Transformer based memory network for sentiment analysis of web comments. *IEEE Access*, 7:179942–179953.

Jockers, M. L. M. (2015). Revealing sentiment and plot arcs with the syuzhet package. (blog), february 2, 2015.

Liu, B., Hu, M., and Cheng, J. (2005). Opinion observer: analyzing and comparing opinions on the web. In *WWW '05: Proceedings of the 14th international conference on World Wide Web*, pages 342–351, New York, NY, USA. ACM.

Liu, B. (2010). Sentiment analysis and subjectivity. *Handbook of natural language processing*, 2(2010):627–666.

Mohammad, S. and Turney, P. (2010). Emotions evoked by common words and phrases: Using mechanical turk to create an emotion lexicon. In *Proceedings of the NAACL HLT 2010 Workshop on Computational Approaches to Analysis and Generation of Emotion in Text*, pages 26–34, Los Angeles, CA, June. Association for Computational Linguistics.

Mohammad, S., Kiritchenko, S., and Zhu, X. (2013). Nrc-canada: Building the state-of-the-art in sentiment analysis of tweets. In *Second Joint Conference on Lexical and Computational Semantics (* SEM), Volume 2: Proceedings of the Seventh International Workshop on Semantic Evaluation (SemEval 2013)*, pages 321–327.

Mohammad, S. M. (2012). From once upon a time to happily ever after: Tracking emotions in mail and books. *Decision Support Systems*, 53(4):730–741.

Mohammad, S. M. (2016). Sentiment analysis: Detecting valence, emotions, and other affectual states from text. In *Emotion measurement*, pages 201–237. Elsevier.

Nielsen, F. A. (2011). A new anew: Evaluation of a word list for sentiment analysis in microblogs. In Matthew Rowe, et al., editors, *MSM*, volume 718 of *CEUR Workshop Proceedings*, pages 93–98. CEUR-WS.org.

Pang, B., Lee, L., et al. (2008). Opinion mining and sentiment analysis. *Foundations and Trends® in Information Retrieval*, 2(1–2):1–135.

Pennington, J., Socher, R., and Manning, C. (2014). Glove: Global vectors for word representation. In *Proceedings of the 2014 Conference on Empirical Methods in Natural Language Processing (EMNLP)*, pages 1532–1543, Doha, Qatar, October. Association for Computational Linguistics.

Reagan, A. J., Mitchell, L., Kiley, D., Danforth, C. M., and Dodds, P. S. (2016). The emotional arcs of stories are dominated by six basic shapes. *EPJ Data Science*, 5(1):31.

Socher, R., Perelygin, A., Wu, J., Chuang, J., Manning, C. D., Ng, A. Y., and Potts, C. (2013). Recursive deep models for semantic compositionality over a sentiment treebank. In *Proceedings of the 2013 conference on empirical methods in natural language processing*, pages 1631–1642.

Tai, K. S., Socher, R., and Manning, C. D. (2015). Improved semantic representations from tree-structured long short-term memory networks. In *Proceedings of the 53rd Annual Meeting of the Association for Computational Linguistics and the 7th International Joint Conference on Natural Language Processing (Volume 1: Long Papers)*, pages 1556–1566.

Vaswani, A., Shazeer, N., Parmar, N., Uszkoreit, J., Jones, L., Gomez, A. N., Kaiser, L. u., and Polosukhin, I. (2017). Attention is all you need. In I. Guyon, et al., editors, *Advances in Neural Information Processing Systems 30*, pages 5998–6008. Curran Associates, Inc.

Whissell, C. M. (1989). The dictionary of affect in language. In *The measurement of emotions*, pages 113–131. Elsevier.

Whissell, C. (2003). Readers' opinions of romantic poetry are consistent with emotional measures based on the dictionary of affect in language. *Perceptual and motor skills*, 96(3):990–992.

Whissell, C. (2010). Whissell's dictionary of affect in language: Technical manual and user's guide. *Laurentian University*.

Zimbra, D., Abbasi, A., Zeng, D., and Chen, H. (2018). The state-of-the-art in twitter sentiment analysis: A review and benchmark evaluation. *ACM Transactions on Management Information Systems (TMIS)*, 9(2):1–29.

9. Language Resource References

Whissell, C. (2010). Whissell's dictionary of affect in language: Technical manual and user's guide. *Laurentian University*.

Workshop on Linguistic and Neurocognitive Resources (LiNCr2020), pages 43–49
Language Resources and Evaluation Conference (LREC 2020), Marseille, 11–16 May 2020

The Little Prince in 26 Languages: Towards a Multilingual Neuro-Cognitive Corpus

Sabrina Stehwien*, Lena Henke*, John T. Hale♠, Jonathan R. Brennan♣, Lars Meyer*
*Max Planck Institute for Human Cognitive and Brain Sciences, Leipzig, DE
♠University of Georgia, Athens, GA, USA
♣University of Michigan, Ann Arbor, MI, USA
{stehwien, henke, lmeyer}@cbs.mpg.de, jthale@uga.edu, jobrenn@umich.edu

Abstract

We present the *Le Petit Prince* Corpus (LPPC), a multi-lingual resource for research in (computational) psycho- and neurolinguistics. The corpus consists of the children's story *The Little Prince* in 26 languages. The dataset is in the process of being built using state-of-the-art methods for speech and language processing and electroencephalography (EEG). The planned release of LPPC dataset will include raw text annotated with dependency graphs in the Universal Dependencies standard, a near-natural-sounding synthetic spoken subset as well as EEG recordings. We will use this corpus for conducting neurolinguistic studies that generalize across a wide range of languages, overcoming typological constraints to traditional approaches. The planned release of the LPPC combines linguistic and EEG data for many languages using fully automatic methods, and thus constitutes a readily extendable resource that supports cross-linguistic and cross-disciplinary research.

1. Introduction

We present the *Le Petit Prince* Corpus (LPPC), a multi-lingual resource for experimental research in cross-linguistic (computational) psycho- and neurolinguistics. The corpus consists of translations of the children's story *Le Petit Prince* (*The Little Prince*), published by Antoine de Saint-Exupéry in 1943, in 26 languages. The corpus is built by combining current methods from speech and language technology, that is, state-of-the-art Text-to-Speech Synthesis (TTS) and dependency parsing, as well as electroencephalography (EEG).

This paper describes ongoing work. We describe the resource that we will release as well as the important aspects to consider while building this corpus. The final release of the dataset will include three main parts: The primary written data is given as raw text and annotated with dependency graphs in the Universal Dependencies (UD) standard (Nivre et al., 2016). A subset of the corpus will be provided as time-aligned synthetic speech. The speech data will be used as an auditory stimulus for recording EEG data, which comprises the final part of the release.

1.1. Motivation

Traditional psycho- and neurolinguistic research has employed factorial experimental designs that require a large number of trials with highly controlled stimuli. Such experimental designs thus limit the generalizability of findings, and it has been increasingly acknowledged in recent years that factorial experiments lack sufficient statistical power and ecological validity (Brennan, 2016; Willems et al., 2015). For this reason, more and more studies rely on naturalistic stimuli (Hamilton and Huth, 2018).

An additional shortcoming of factorial experiments is evident from recent findings in probabilistic language processing: Repetitive presentation of large numbers of matched stimuli can have the undesired effect of changing transitional probabilities during the experiment and thus, of obscuring neurobiological results (Kroczek and Gunter, 2017). The development of information-theoretic quantifications of speech and language processing (Hale, 2001) and their excellent fit to behavioral (Levy, 2008; Demberg and Keller, 2008) and neurobiological data (Hale et al., 2018; Rabovsky et al., 2018; Frank et al., 2015) supports this.

Traditional psycho- and neurolinguistic studies have typically been restricted to single or few individual languages. This results in limited generalizability beyond small typological domains, thereby hindering the understanding of cross-linguistic commonalities and differences in the cognitive apparatus and neural substrate of speech and language processing (Kandylaki and Bornkessel-Schlesewsky, 2019).

In contrast, the LPPC as a resource facilitates generalization across a range of languages (Kandylaki and Bornkessel-Schlesewsky, 2019), helping the psycho- and neurolinguistic fields to further overcome their current statistical and typological limitations. The motivation for building this dataset is in line with the recent development of openly accessible naturalistic stimulus sets in the neurolinguistic community, such as the *Mother of All Unification Studies* (Schoffelen et al., 2019), the *Narrative Brain Dataset* (Lopopolo et al., 2018), the *Alice Datasets* (Bhattasali et al., 2020) and the ongoing *Alice in Language Localizer Wonderland* project[1]. Unlike factorial and/or monolingual experimental datasets that are tailored to just one specific question, the LPPC's lexico-syntactic annotation in the UD standard fosters research that addresses a broad range of linguistic research questions. The LPPC is also sustainable in that its data is amenable to future re-analysis that addresses future research questions. Furthermore, the use of the dataset will facilitate the formulation of neurobiological frameworks that generalize across languages (Bornkessel-Schlesewsky and Schlesewsky, 2016), assuming that the structural and functional properties of the human brain that subserve language are shared among speakers of all languages (Futrell et al., 2015; Levy, 2008; Brennan et al., 2019). In turn, the dataset may also serve as re-

[1] https://evlab.mit.edu/alice

source for traditional linguistic research that aims to explain why languages are different, yet they all can be processed by brains that are unitary across humans.

1.2. The LPPC – an automatic corpus

Recent advancements in the field of speech and language processing, fueled by the striking success of deep learning models, have made it feasible to automatically create and annotate large amounts of data with a higher quality than previously possible. We exploit such methods for building our resource, that, given it comprises 26 languages, would require much effort using traditional manual methods. Apart from the primary text data, which is manually cleaned, the database is created using automatic dependency parsing, forced-alignment and speech synthesis. In addition to the state-of-the-art speech and language processing tools employed for building the corpus, the EEG data is preprocessed using a fully automatic pipeline setup. We are also planning to make the EEG data available to the community in an open format that facilitates further processing. To the best of our knowledge, the LPPC is the first resource for neurolinguistic research that is not only created by, but also combines such methods.

2. The LPPC multi-lingual resource

The corpus consists of translations of the children's story *Le Petit Prince* by Antoine de Saint-Exupéry. The text was originally written in 1943 and has since been translated into over 300 languages[2].

The languages chosen for the LPPC are Arabic, Chinese (Mandarin), Czech, Danish, Dutch, English, Finnish, French, German, Greek, Hindi, Hungarian, Indonesian, Italian, Japanese, Korean, Norwegian, Polish, Portuguese, Russian, Slovak, Spanish, Swedish, Turkish, Ukrainian, and Vietnamese.

The criteria for choosing these languages was their availability both as a significantly large treebank in the UD treebank (Nivre et al., 2016) (to allow for uniform syntactic parsing across languages) as well as in Google's Text-to-Speech API[3] voice selection. Both tools are part of automatic pipelines for creating the linguistic annotations and the speech data, respectively.

2.1. Primary written data

The primary data in the LPPC consists of one text version of the story in each of 26 chosen languages. The full story comprises 27 chapters in total (plus a short prologue) and the English version amounts to roughly 16k words. The LPPC includes the first six chapters in each language as spoken data, amounting to around 20 minutes of speech ($\approx$ 250 sentences).

We chose existing published translations of the story. Since the domain of the data is literary text, the versions for the various languages cannot be expected to be translated directly at the sentence level. Furthermore, we do not have any control on how close the different translations are to the French original, and we expect expect a certain degree of variation between the different translations. Nevertheless, given the fact that the book follows a clear story line and uses rather simple language, we consider the translations to be fairly parallel. The LPPC is therefore not a strictly parallel corpus, but a combination of comparable parts as well as parallel, but unaligned sentences[4].

2.1.1. Acquisition of text

For the written text part of the corpus, we acquired electronic translations of the text. In most languages, multiple translations have been published since the first issue, and newer translations continue to appear until today. Therefore, we carefully chose versions according to the following criteria: The first being the availability as an e-book[5], as these are readily obtained and easily converted to raw text. The second criterion was the availability of bibliographic data. Since the texts available on web differ in quality, we selected releases that contained information on the translator, year, and publishing house. We also discussed the choice of text with native speakers in cases where we were unsure about the quality of the translated versions.

2.1.2. Choice of translation

We placed an additional constraint on our choice of translations based on diachronic linguistic changes that may pose additional interfering factors during neuroscientific studies. Such problems may arise, for example, when performing EEG studies on canonical participant samples, e.g. in an age range of 20 to 30 years. Since participants in this age group are less familiar with the writing style used in the original version from 1943 and the early translations, we chose to collect more recent translations for the corpus. This decision was based on the outdated language in older translations, which may confound experimental measurements. For example, the Hungarian version uses the obsolete term *fölnőtt* for the word *grown-up*, whereas the new version uses *felnőtt*. An additional concern was the use of literary writing style, which has changed considerably over the years. Old words or syntactic constructions may be unfamiliar to participants and thus be experienced as unusual, thereby triggering meta-cognitive processing.

Conversely, due to the fact that *Le Petit Prince* is a well-known text, we expect that participants who are very familiar with the original translations may also display interference effects when confronted with a different translation. Therefore, this choice comprises a trade-off between a familiar story and a contemporary language style. To keep the corpus as consistent as possible, however, we chose the newest translation available that fits the aforementioned criteria. Apart from the French original text, the full collection therefore contains translations that were published after the

[2]It has thus been referred to as the most-translated non-religious text in the world (Le Figaro, 7. April 2017).

[3]https://cloud.google.com/text-to-speech/

[4]Cross-language sentence alignments may be carried out by hand to a limited extent. The research questions we seek to address with this corpus, discussed in section 3.3.3. do not require a strictly parallel corpus, and we therefore do not plan to include such alignments in this release.

[5]Obtaining digitized text from print versions was deemed too error-prone due to expected issues in using optical character recognition (OCR).

year 2000 except for Russian and Slovak, for which such recent translations are currently not available as e-books.

2.1.3. Preprocessing

In order to prepare the written text for the annotation pipeline, the documents needed to be cleaned of formatting errors, punctuation, typographical errors and other inconsistencies resulting from the conversion process. Additional text stemming from the title page, picture captions as well as biography sections or other supplemental sections was removed. Each sentence of the text is assigned a separate ID to facilitate further processing. We employed native speakers to preprocess and check the texts manually.

2.2. Synthesized speech data

The first six chapters of the story will be converted to spoken language via Text-to-Speech Synthesis (TTS). We chose to use synthetic voices over natural voices for two main reasons: First, due to the time and cost involved in recording professional speakers in a laboratory setting. Second, to have more control over the resulting speech output and to obtain voices that do not differ too much in voice quality, pitch and speaking rate. This allows for better experimental control over the effects of individual voice differences during neuroscientific studies.

2.2.1. Google Text-to-Speech API

In order to obtain synthesized speech that is as natural as possible, we chose to use the state-of-the-art WaveNet (Oord et al., 2016) voices provided by the Google Cloud Text-to-Speech API. We chose this synthesizer since it currently provides the largest selection of natural sounding voices. The client libraries are an efficient method of creating speech output in a wide range of languages in human-like quality. The API also allows the input to be further enhanced using the W3C Speech Synthesis Markup Language (SSML[6]), which enables the user to manually add additional instructions on how the input text is to be synthesized. The Google API supports a subset of SSML tags for generating different prosody or for reading out numerals.

2.2.2. Manual markup of input text

The first six chapters as cleaned written text files are used as raw input for TTS. The text is segmented into smaller parts, that is, single sentences or paragraphs, for easier handling during the processing pipeline.

We recruited native speakers with expertise in TTS to create SSML markup that increase the naturalness of the synthesis where necessary. This markup can be used to change the prosody, for example for making pitch modifications and inserting breaks. An example of the markup is illustrated in Figure 1.

Since the prosody across sentence boundaries can differ when sentences are entered individually or as part of a longer text, they were also asked to decide whether to synthesize the sentences individually or as grouped into paragraphs. The sentence IDs assigned to the raw text are kept track of during this step.

We let the native speakers choose the most natural sounding female WaveNet voices according to their opinion. The only current exception is Spanish, for which currently only one "standard" female voice is provided.

2.2.3. Naturalness of synthetic speech

The naturalness of the speech recordings is constrained by feasibility: Based on prior experiences, we chose to employ TTS because the recruitment of professional speakers of comparable professionalism, speech training, and speech quality across languages is a hard-to-predict risk to a project of this size and scope. However, we ensured that the synthetic voices chosen for this corpus are of very high, and in part near-natural, quality. The mean opinion scores (MOS) obtained by using a WaveNet vocoder in the TTS system have been reported to greatly surpass those of traditional parametric or concatenative TTS systems (Shen et al., 2018; Oord et al., 2016).

In addition, we take two further measures to handle variability in synthesis quality: First, the native speakers in charge of SSML adjustment will report gross problems with the TTS output and SSML markup, such that corpus users can easily identify sentences of low synthesis quality. Second, we plan to include with each sentence the results of a rating study collected via crowdsourcing (e.g. Amazon Mechanical Turk), allowing users of the LPPC to include parametric covariates of naturalness in their statistical models or define individual naturalness thresholds.

2.2.4. Alignment of speech and text

The text and speech data will be time-aligned, that is, the timestamps that denote the start and end times of each word in the text will be automatically obtained and provided with the corpus. This step is especially necessary for aligning the spoken part of the data to the EEG recordings.

While standard available tools generally yield good performance in resource-rich languages such as English and German, we expect a poorer quality of the alignments in other languages, and that for certain languages there may not even exist suitable tools. Since Google's services do not provide timestamps for the synthesized output, we will use a workaround solution[7] using their multi-lingual Speech-To-Text API[8], which does provide word offset times.

2.3. Lexico-syntactic annotations

The LPPC will contain lexico-syntactic annotations for the written text part of the corpus that we will automatically obtain using natural language processing (NLP) tools. The full texts will be parsed according to the UD framework. This framework comprises a method of combining consistent annotations across languages. Furthermore, previous evidence has suggested a link between syntactic dependency and psycholinguistic processing (Brennan et al., 2019). The parsed output will be provided in a standard format (CoNLL), which includes part-of-speech (POS) tags and lemmatization. We will train the best state-of-the-art parser trained on the respective UD treebank for each lan-

[6]https://www.w3.org/TR/speech-synthesis11/

[7]This workaround had been suggested to us by Google.

[8]https://cloud.google.com/speech-to-text

```
<p>
  <s> He bent over the drawing. </s><break time="300ms"/>
  <s><prosody pitch="+2st" rate="110%"> "Not so small as all that. <break time="500ms"/>
   Look! <break time="300ms"/> He's gone to sleep!" </prosody></s><break time="700ms"/>
  <s> And that's how I made the acquaintance of the little prince. </s>
</p>
```

Figure 1: Example paragraph taken from the English translation of *Le Petit Prince* with SSML markup

guage for parsing. We refer to section 3.3.2. for a discussion on annotation quality estimation.

2.4. EEG data

We aim to collect EEG recordings from 20 participants for each of the languages in the LPPC. During EEG recording, the synthesized speech data (i.e., the first six chapters of the story) will be played via loudspeakers at a volume that is comfortable to the participants. To ensure that participants stay alert and focus on the content of the story, a set of multiple-choice comprehension questions will be asked after each chapter; questions and responses will be included in the corpus. This also enables corpus users to model inter-individual comprehension differences or define their own selection thresholds.

While we plan to include an active task, the paradigm behind the planned EEG recordings is mostly passive. We refer to a body of literature from the speech, language, and music fields (Cheung et al., 2019; Hale et al., 2018; Rabovsky et al., 2018; Frank et al., 2015; Armeni et al., 2019; Brennan and Martin, 2020; Weissbart et al., 2020; Meyer and Gumbert, 2018; Di Liberto et al., 2015) to expect variability of electrophysiological responses of interest to the user (e.g., evoked responses, changes in oscillatory phase and power) to exhibit enough variance for state-of-the-art statistical analysis (e.g., multiple regression, temporal response functions, speech–brain-coupling measures).

EEG data will be continuously recorded from 64 electrodes.The setup will be referenced against the left mastoid and grounded to the sternum. To facilitate subtraction of eye blink and movement artifacts, the horizontal and vertical electrooculograms will be acquired. Scalp electrodes will be placed according to the 10–20 system in an elastic cap. During recording, the word start and end markers of the audio will be stored as events in the EEG file.

Artifact cleaning will be automatic, combining functions from EEGLAB (Delorme and Makeig, 2004) and FieldTrip (Oostenveld et al., 2011) running in MATLAB®. We will use an absolute threshold to remove outlier recording channels. The 50-Hz artifact and resonance frequencies will be projected out via a combination of a perfect-reconstruction filter bank and a spatial filter (de Cheveigné, 2019). Remaining artifacts will be removed using independent-components analysis (ICA). To stabilize ICA, an 1-Hz highpass filter will be applied (Winkler et al., 2015), followed by wavelet ICA (Gabard-Durnam et al., 2018) and ICA (Makeig et al., 1996); artifact components will be automatically classified using MARA (Winkler et al., 2011), ADJUST (Mognon et al., 2011), and ICLABEL (Pion-Tonachini et al., 2019). Artifactual components will be removed from the data highpass-filtered at 0.01 Hz (Winkler et al., 2015). Then, channels removed from the initial thresholding will be interpolated.

3. Ongoing work

We are currently in the stage of acquiring cleaned versions of the text data as well as the SSML markup as input for our speech processing pipeline. The annotation of the text data and the recording of EEG data will occur in parallel once the acquisition of the primary data is completed.

3.1. Availability

We plan to release the corpus in three stages: (1) The release of the primary text data, synthesized speech and (word-level) time-alignments, (2) the lexico-syntactic annotations of the written text, and (3) the preprocessed EEG data recorded during listening and aligned with the speech data. The first version of the corpus release is expected to be available in parallel to this publication. The release of neuroimaging data is postponed for the third release due to pending legal issues regarding data privacy[9]. We plan to make as many EEG recordings available as possible under these constraints. For better re-usability, we also aim to convert the EEG data to openNeuro[10] format.

3.2. Metadata

The corpus release will include bibliographical information on the e-book publications (e.g., name of the translator, year of publication, and publishing house). We will provide the Google WaveNet voice ID as well as the SSML markup used to create the synthesized speech data. We will also provide detailed information on the NLP tools and methods used to create the lexico-syntactic annotations, as well as information on the estimated quality for each language. The EEG subset of the corpus will include metadata such as the age, gender, native language and bilinguality of each subject. Complete EEG metadata (e.g., filter and ICA settings) will be provided with the respective release.

3.3. Discussion

Due to use of automatic annotation methods and the choice of using synthesized speech for our corpus, several open questions arise, which we discuss in the following. Furthermore, we welcome feedback on possible additional caveats and extensions while the corpus is under construction.

In addition, by means of an outlook, we will discuss some classes of research avenues that could be addressed by employing the LPPC in planned typological contrasts.

[9]Subjects must give written consent according to the European General Data Protection Regulation (GDPR).

[10]https://openneuro.org/

Corpus subset	Size	Annotations	Metadata
Text	27 chapters, $\approx$ 16k English words	Universal Dependencies	bibliographical data, NLP tools
Speech	chapters 1–6, $\approx$ 20 minutes of speech	time-alignments	Google voice, SSML
EEG	speech subset	time-alignments	subject metadata

Table 1: Overview of the planned LPPC resource in 26 languages.

3.3.1. Use of synthesized speech

The decision to use TTS to create the speech part of the LPPC was based on our aim to use the dataset for neurolinguistic studies that focus on higher-level syntactic processing. We would like to stress that we do not recommend the corpus for research on lower-level phonetic or auditory processing, since these would require human speech to rule out any confounds created by parts of the auditory stimulus that may be perceived as clearly non-human.

As discussed in section 2.2.3., the Google voices used to create the spoken part of the corpus have been judged to be of significantly higher quality than the best previous TTS systems and the SSML markup is used to further increase the naturalness of the synthesized speech. However, the synthesized speech still differs from human speech, especially when used to read out a literary text. We had chosen this method despite this drawback due to the fact that it enables us to efficiently obtain speech data for all chosen languages.

Depending on the outcome of the ratings obtained from crowdsourcing (see 2.2.3.), it may be necessary to include a recording of a human speaker for at least one language to perform a comparison in further neuroscientific studies. Expanding the selection of languages which include human speech can then be taken into account for possible future versions of the corpus.

3.3.2. Quality of automatic annotations

Since the linguistic annotations will be obtained using purely automatic NLP methods, they are expected to include errors. While the quality of the automatic time-alignments and the syntactic parses will likely be quite high for resource-rich languages such as English, we expect a higher degree of error in low-resource languages. By using tools that can be applied cross-linguistically, however, we aim to generate annotations with a high accuracy. Furthermore, domain differences between the data used to train the tools and the LPPC (children's literature) can be reduced by choosing treebanks from literary texts. The exact choice of tools is subject to current work and will consist of methods that meet this aim.

Possible methods to increase the quality of the linguistic annotations include hand-annotating small amounts of text as a gold-standard reference for automatic evaluation and for domain adaptation of annotation models, or employing native speakers to perform manual corrections in cases where the error rate is deemed too large to be acceptable. Previous efforts to increase the quality of automatic corpus annotation include, for example, a silver standard approach (Rebholz-Schuhmann et al., 2010; Schweitzer et al., 2018; Hale et al., 2019), in which several annotation layers can be combined to estimate confidence scores.

3.3.3. Outlook: an EEG typology

The main motivation for building the LPPC is to address the notion of overcoming the typological restrictedness of prior and current experimental designs in psycho- and neurolinguistics, which is a major obstacle for the generalizability of cognitive and neuroanatomical frameworks of language comprehension (Kandylaki and Bornkessel-Schlesewsky, 2019). While this work-in-progress paper cannot serve the purpose of providing an exhaustive list of cross-linguistic contrastive research questions, we here give a short set for inspiration.

First, cross-linguistic variance in evoked potentials and oscillatory power and phase changes associated with memory storage mechanisms of dependency formation could be tested (Meyer et al., 2013; Kluender and Kutas, 1993). Initial pilot work supports the feasibility of this (Brennan et al., 2019). Moreover, further open questions of models of dependency formation could be tested cross-linguistically, including retrieval cues and their weighting, as well as whether memory retrieval is activation-based or direct (Vasishth et al., 2019; McElree, 2000). Indeed, it has been shown that such fine-grained aspects can be dissociated; for instance, Search Effort as formalized in parsing algorithms was shown to model evoked components classically associated with syntactic processing difficulty (Hale et al., 2018). In addition to enhancing the validity of parsing algorithms proper from their statistical fit to the underlying electrophysiology, seminal work on the alignment between electrophysiological excitability and information content (Weissbart et al., 2020; Meyer and Gumbert, 2018) could be tested for its cross-linguistic generalizability, thus working towards an information-theoretic typology (Hahn et al., 2020; Gibson et al., 2019).

4. Conclusion

In this paper, we have presented the LPPC as a resource that combines linguistic data in the form of text and speech with EEG data for 26 languages. The corpus is currently being built semi-automatically; only the written story was acquired and the text cleaned by hand, and the synthetic speech data, linguistic annotations as well as EEG data is obtained using automatic state-of-the-art tools and methods. The LPPC bridges several gaps between traditional psycho- and neurolinguistic approaches and current data-driven research and enables researchers to investigate and generalize research questions across a wide range of languages. We hope to show that using corpora obtained using automatic methods is a realistic alternative to manual naturalistic stimuli, since this approach enables testing larger amounts of data and across a broader range of languages.

The corpus is work-in-progress. Apart from the planned release described here, we encourage future extensions of the corpus by the (computational) psycho- and neurolinguistics communities to include additional languages as they become available in Google's TTS voice selection or in other synthesis systems of comparable quality. Furthermore, the speech part of the LPPC is limited to the first 6 chapters. Provided that the quality of the output is acceptable and that it proves to be a useful resource, the speech part can readily be extended.

As future work, we plan to further expand the scope of research questions that can be addressed with the LPPC by incorporating data from additional neuroimaging modalities, such as magnetoencephalography (MEG) and functional magnetic resonance imaging (fMRI; see Bhattasali et al. (2019) for an application using human speech). Our vision is for the LPPC to become an open infrastructure to which researchers from various communities can contribute by adding further modalities, such as functional near-infrared spectroscopy or electrocorticography. We also welcome further suggestions and contributions to help expand the utility of the LPPC across disciplines to facilitate innovative psycho- and neurolinguistic research.

5. Acknowledgements

The authors would like to thank Joakim Nivre for helpful discussion. Monique Horstmann carried out preparatory work during early stages. This work was funded by the Max Planck Society through the award of Max Planck Research Group *Language Cycles* to Lars Meyer.

6. Bibliographical References

Armeni, K., Willems, R. M., Van den Bosch, A., and Schoffelen, J.-M. (2019). Frequency-specific brain dynamics related to prediction during language comprehension. *NeuroImage*, 198:283–295.

Bhattasali, S., Fabre, M., Luh, W.-M., Al Saied, H., Constant, M., Pallier, C., Brennan, J. R., Spreng, R. N., and Hale, J. (2019). Localising memory retrieval and syntactic composition: an fMRI study of naturalistic language comprehension. *Language, Cognition and Neuroscience*, 34(4):491–510.

Bhattasali, S., Brennan, J. R., Luh, W.-M., Franzluebbers, B., and Hale, J. T. (2020). The Alice Datasets: fMRI EEG observations of natural language comprehension. In *Proceedings of the Eleventh International Conference on Language Resources and Evaluation (LREC 2020)*, Marseille, France, May. European Language Resources Association (ELRA).

Bornkessel-Schlesewsky, I. and Schlesewsky, M. (2016). The importance of linguistic typology for the neurobiology of language. *Linguistic Typology*, 20(3):615–621.

Brennan, J. R. and Martin, A. E. (2020). Phase synchronization varies systematically with linguistic structure composition. *Philosophical Transactions of the Royal Society B*, 375(1791):20190305.

Brennan, J., Martin, A. E., Dunagan, D., Meyer, L., and Hale, J. (2019). Resolving dependencies during naturalistic listening. In *11th Annual Meeting of the Society for the Neurobiology of Language*.

Brennan, J. (2016). Naturalistic sentence comprehension in the brain. *Language and Linguistics Compass*, 10(7):299–313.

Cheung, V. K., Harrison, P. M., Meyer, L., Pearce, M. T., Haynes, J.-D., and Koelsch, S. (2019). Uncertainty and surprise jointly predict musical pleasure and amygdala, hippocampus, and auditory cortex activity. *Current Biology*, 29(23):4084–4092.

de Cheveigné, A. (2019). ZapLine: a simple and effective method to remove power line artifacts. *NeuroImage*.

Delorme, A. and Makeig, S. (2004). Eeglab: an open source toolbox for analysis of single-trial eeg dynamics including independent component analysis. *Journal of neuroscience methods*, 134(1):9–21.

Demberg, V. and Keller, F. (2008). Data from eye-tracking corpora as evidence for theories of syntactic processing complexity. *Cognition*, 109(2):193–210.

Di Liberto, G. M., O'Sullivan, J. A., and Lalor, E. C. (2015). Low-frequency cortical entrainment to speech reflects phoneme-level processing. *Current Biology*, 25(19):2457–2465.

Frank, S. L., Otten, L. J., Galli, G., and Vigliocco, G. (2015). The ERP response to the amount of information conveyed by words in sentences. *Brain and Language*, 140:1–11.

Futrell, R., Mahowald, K., and Gibson, E. (2015). Large-scale evidence of dependency length minimization in 37 languages. *Proceedings of the National Academy of Sciences of the United States of America*, 112(33):10336–10341.

Gabard-Durnam, L. J., Mendez Leal, A. S., Wilkinson, C. L., and Levin, A. R. (2018). The harvard automated processing pipeline for electroencephalography (happe): standardized processing software for developmental and high-artifact data. *Frontiers in neuroscience*, 12:97.

Gibson, E., Futrell, R., Piandadosi, S. T., Dautriche, I., Mahowald, K., Bergen, L., and Levy, R. (2019). How efficiency shapes human language. *Trends in cognitive sciences*.

Hahn, M., Jurafsky, D., and Futrell, R. (2020). Universals of word order reflect optimization of grammars for efficient communication. *Proceedings of the National Academy of Sciences*, 117(5):2347–2353.

Hale, J., Dyer, C., Kuncoro, A., Brennan, J. R., and Acl, A. (2018). Finding Syntax in Human Encephalography with Beam Search. In *ACL*, pages 1–9.

Hale, J., Kuncoro, A., Hall, K., Dyer, C., and Brennan, J. (2019). Text genre and training data size in human-like parsing. In *Proceedings of the 2019 Conference on Empirical Methods in Natural Language Processing and the 9th International Joint Conference on Natural Language Processing (EMNLP-IJCNLP)*, pages 5846–5852, Hong Kong, China, November. Association for Computational Linguistics.

Hale, J. (2001). A probabilistic Earley parser as a psycholinguistic model. In *Proceedings of the second meeting of the North American Chapter of the Association for Computational Linguistics on Language technologies*, pages 1–8. Association for Computational Linguistics.

Hamilton, L. S. and Huth, A. G. (2018). The revolution will not be controlled: natural stimuli in speech neuroscience. *Language, Cognition and Neuroscience*, 0(0):1–10.

Kandylaki, K. D. and Bornkessel-Schlesewsky, I. (2019). From story comprehension to the neurobiology of language. *Language, Cognition and Neuroscience*, 4(4):405–410.

Kluender, R. and Kutas, M. (1993). Bridging the gap: Evidence from erps on the processing of unbounded dependencies. *Journal of Cognitive Neuroscience*, 5(2):196–214.

Kroczek, L. O. and Gunter, T. C. (2017). Communicative predictions can overrule linguistic priors. *Scientific reports*, 7(1):1–9.

Levy, R. (2008). Expectation-based syntactic comprehension. *Cognition*, 106(3):1126–1177.

Lopopolo, A., Frank, S. L., Van den Bosch, A., Nijhof, A., and Willems, R. M. (2018). The Narrative Brain Dataset (NBD), an fMRI dataset for the study of natural language processing in the brain.

Makeig, S., Bell, A. J., Jung, T.-P., and Sejnowski, T. J. (1996). Independent component analysis of electroencephalographic data. In D S Touretzky, et al., editors, *Advances in neural information processing systems 8*, pages 145–151. MIT Press, Cambridge.

McElree, B. (2000). Sentence comprehension is mediated by content-addressable memory structures. *Journal of psycholinguistic research*, 29(2):111–123.

Meyer, L. and Gumbert, M. (2018). Synchronization of electrophysiological responses with speech benefits syntactic information processing. *Journal of cognitive neuroscience*, 30(8):1066–1074.

Meyer, L., Obleser, J., and Friederici, A. D. (2013). Left parietal alpha enhancement during working memory-intensive sentence processing. *Cortex*, 49(3):711–721.

Mognon, A., Jovicich, J., Bruzzone, L., and Buiatti, M. (2011). ADJUST: An automatic EEG artifact detector based on the joint use of spatial and temporal features. *Psychophysiology*, 48(2):229–240.

Nivre, J., De Marneffe, M.-C., Ginter, F., Goldberg, Y., Hajic, J., Manning, C. D., McDonald, R., Petrov, S., Pyysalo, S., Silveira, N., et al. (2016). Universal dependencies v1: A multilingual treebank collection. In *Proceedings of the Tenth International Conference on Language Resources and Evaluation (LREC'16)*, pages 1659–1666.

Oord, A. v. d., Dieleman, S., Zen, H., Simonyan, K., Vinyals, O., Graves, A., Kalchbrenner, N., Senior, A., and Kavukcuoglu, K. (2016). Wavenet: A generative model for raw audio. *arXiv preprint arXiv:1609.03499*.

Oostenveld, R., Fries, P., Maris, E., and Schoffelen, J. M. (2011). FieldTrip: open source software for advanced analysis of MEG, EEG, and invasive electrophysiological data. *Computational Intelligence and Neuroscience*, 2011:156869.

Pion-Tonachini, L., Kreutz-Delgado, K., and Makeig, S. (2019). Iclabel: An automated electroencephalographic independent component classifier, dataset, and website. *NeuroImage*, 198:181–197.

Rabovsky, M., Hansen, S. S., and McClelland, J. L. (2018). Modelling the N400 brain potential as change in a probabilistic representation of meaning. *Nature Human Behaviour*, 2(9):693–705.

Rebholz-Schuhmann, D., Jimeno-Yepes, A. J., van Mulligen, E. M., Kang, N., Kors, J., Milward, D., Corbett, P., Buyko, E., Tomanek, K., Beisswanger, E., and Hahn, U. (2010). The calbc silver standard corpus for biomedical named entities — a study in harmonizing the contributions from four independent named entity taggers. In *Proceedings of the Seventh International Conference on Language Resources and Evaluation (LREC'10)*, Valletta, Malta.

Schoffelen, J.-M., Oostenveld, R., Lam, N. H., Uddén, J., Hultén, A., and Hagoort, P. (2019). A 204-subject multimodal neuroimaging dataset to study language processing. *Scientific data*, 6(1):1–13.

Schweitzer, K., Eckart, K., Gärtner, M., Falenska, A., Riester, A., Roesiger, I., Schweitzer, A., Stehwien, S., and Kuhn, J. (2018). German Radio Interviews: The GRAIN Release of the SFB732 Silver Standard Collection. In *Proceedings of the Eleventh International Conference on Language Resources and Evaluation (LREC 2018)*, Miyazaki, Japan, May 7-12, 2018.

Shen, J., Pang, R., Weiss, R. J., Schuster, M., Jaitly, N., Yang, Z., Chen, Z., Zhang, Y., Wang, Y., Skerrv-Ryan, R., Saurous, R. A., Agiomvrgiannakis, Y., and Wu, Y. (2018). Natural TTS synthesis by conditioning Wavenet on Mel spectrogram predictions. In *2018 IEEE International Conference on Acoustics, Speech and Signal Processing (ICASSP)*, pages 4779–4783.

Vasishth, S., Nicenboim, B., Engelmann, F., and Burchert, F. (2019). Computational models of retrieval processes in sentence processing. *Trends in cognitive sciences*.

Weissbart, H., Kandylaki, K. D., and Reichenbach, T. (2020). Cortical tracking of surprisal during continuous speech comprehension. *Journal of cognitive neuroscience*, 32(1):155–166.

Willems, R. M., Frank, S. L., Nijhof, A. D., Hagoort, P., and Van den Bosch, A. (2015). Prediction during natural language comprehension. *Cerebral Cortex*, 26(6):2506–2516.

Winkler, I., Haufe, S., and Tangermann, M. (2011). Automatic classification of artifactual ica-components for artifact removal in eeg signals. *Behavioral and Brain Functions*, 7(1):30.

Winkler, I., Debener, S., Muller, K. R., and Tangermann, M. (2015). On the influence of high-pass filtering on ICA-based artifact reduction in EEG-ERP. In *Proceedings of the Annual International Conference of the IEEE Engineering in Medicine and Biology Society, EMBS*, volume 2015-Novem, pages 4101–4105. IEEE.

Workshop on Linguistic and Neurocognitive Resources (LiNCr2020), pages 50–58
Language Resources and Evaluation Conference (LREC 2020), Marseille, 11–16 May 2020

Towards a Multi-Dataset for Complex Emotions Learning based on Deep Neural Networks

Belainine Billal, Sadat Fatiha, Boukadoum Mounir, Lounis Hakim
Computer Science, UQAM, Quebec, Canada
belainine.billal@courrier.uqam.ca,
{sadat.fatiha,boukadoum.mounir, lounis.hakim}@uqam.ca

Abstract

In sentiment analysis, several researchers have used emoji and hashtags as specific forms of training and supervision. Some emotions, such as fear and disgust, are underrepresented in the text of social media. Others, such as anticipation, are absent. This research paper proposes a new dataset for complex emotion detection using a combination of several existing corpora in order to represent and interpret complex emotions based on the Plutchik's theory. Our experiments and evaluations confirm that using Transfer Learning (TL) with a rich emotional corpus, facilitates the detection of complex emotions in a four-dimensional space. In addition, the incorporation of the rule on the reverse emotions in the model's architecture brings a significant improvement in terms of precision, recall, and F-score.

Keywords: Complex Emotions, Emotional Intelligence, Data Augmentation, Machine Learning, Natural Language Processing

1. Introduction

Several works in natural language processing (NLP) have addressed the recognition of expression of emotions. They can be divided into two approaches. The first one assesses emotions by using quantitative metrics such as the level of intensity or valence, arousal, domination, etc. For example, the emotion carried by a text is measured as very joyful, a little angry, fearful, etc., with the metric value referring to the degree of emotion (Posner et al., 2005). The second approach starts from a dictionary of basic emotions, considered as atomic and irreducible, to build more complex ones. This is the case of the Plutchik model (Plutchik, 1980), which allows to represent a complex emotion as a combination of several basic emotions (De Bonis, 1996).

Regardless of the approach used, a relevant corpus of examples is required for training and/or validation.
Many researchers have considered social media with emoji and hashtags as a source of training data. However, Some emotions, such as fear and disgust, are underrepresented in those media, and others such as anticipation are absent.

This research proposes the following contributions:

1. Construction of a novel annotated dataset for emotion-related work, created by mixing several existing corpora, that addresses the previous limitations. This annotated corpus is then used in a system designed to detect complex emotions based on the Plutchik model.

2. Introduction of a formal method for reading and interpreting complex emotions based on basic emotion vectors. This vector is reduced in a 4-dimensional space.

3. Introduction of a rule for reverse emotions in the model's architecture, stating that an emotion cannot be present at the same time as its opposite.

The structure of the present paper is described as follows: Section 2. introduces the Plutchik model in the context of this study, Section 3. surveys the state of the art on the analysis and detection of emotions, Section 4. describes our approach to the recognition of complex emotions with a deep neural network, Sections 5. and 6. describe the experiments that help evaluate our model and compare its performance to other models, along with an error analysis and a discussion. Finally, Section 7. concludes this work and offers perspectives for future research.

2. Overview of the Plutchik Theory

Plutchik (Plutchik, 2003) proposed a model based on a dictionary of emotions similar to the color dictionary. Indeed, since there are secondary colors derived from primary colors, there would be secondary emotions derived from primary emotions, and each combination of certain primary emotions can generate secondary emotions (Plutchik, 1980).
According to Plutchik (Plutchik, 1980), there are four pairs of opposite emotions: *(Joy, Sadness), (Trust, Disgust), (Fear, Anger), (Surprise, Anticipation)*. The eight dimensions of these fundamental emotions are adjacent and arranged like a cone, with the terms that designate the maximum intensity of each emotion at the top.
In relation to complex emotions that are added to the primary ones, first we can find the emotions that are a result of the combination of two adjacent emotions. These are the primary dyads (Plutchik, 2003). Moreover, there are emotions that are the result of a combination of two adjacent primary emotions, but separated by an emotion. These are the secondary dyads. Finally, the emotions that are the result of a combination of two adjacent primary emotions, but separated by two emotions, these are the tertiary dyads (Plutchik, 1980). Table 1 represents all possible combinations of the primary dyads, the secondary dyads, as well as the tertiary dyads, with the generated emotions according to the Plutchik model.

Primary Dyads	Results	Secondary Dyads	Results	Tertiary Dyads	Results
Joy + Trust	Love	Joy + Fear	Guilt	Surprise + Joy	Delight
Trust + Fear	Submission	Surprise + Trust	Curiosity	Sadness + Trust	Faintness
Surprise + Fear	Alarm	Sadness + Fear	Despair	Disgust + Fear	Shame
Surprise + Sadness	Disappointment	Surprise + Disgust	Horror	Surprise + Anger	Outrage
Sadness + Disgust	Remorse	Sadness + Anger	Envy	Sadness + Anticipation	Pessimism
Disgust + Anger	Contempt	Disgust + Anticipation	Cynicism	Disgust + Joy	Morbidity
Anticipation + Anger	Aggressiveness	Anger + Joy	Pride	Anger + Trust	Domination
Anticipation + Joy	Optimism	Anticipation + Trust	Fatalism	Anticipation + Fear	Anxiety

Table 1: Combinations of Plutchik's emotions (Plutchik, 2003).

3. Related Work

Because of the absence of annotated data, manually or otherwise, many NLP tasks related to sentiment analysis and emotion mining use co-occurring emotional expressions for remote supervision of social media, to allow models to learn directly useful textual representations before modelling these tasks (Mohammad et al., 2013; Nida et al., 2019).

3.1. Previous works on emotion recognition

Some works use binarized emojis as noisy labels (Read, 2005; Nakov et al., 2016; Yang et al., 2016; Nikhil and Srivastava, 2018), but emojis can be ambiguous as they can serve both as comments or to set emotional state of a text. This ambiguity was addresses by Kunneman et al. (2014) with emotional hashtags such as *#nice* and *#lame*. Nevertheless, DeepMoji has succeeded in showing that emoticons can be used to accurately categorize the emotional content of texts in many cases (Felbo et al., 2017). But DeepMoji requires more than one billion pieces of data for training (1 246 million of tweets), and it has two limitations: a) The analyzed text must contain emoticons; b) the emojis do not always reflect the emotional state behind the writing of the text, since they can also be used to complete the writing text.Other works use emotion theories such as Ekman's six basic emotions and Plutchik's eight basic emotions (Mohammad et al., 2013; Suttles and Ide, 2013; Felbo et al., 2017). The categorization is also done manually, and it requires requires an understanding of the emotional content of each expression, which is difficult and time-consuming for sophisticated combinations of emotional content.

The work of Suttles and Ide (2013) uses a binary classifier that indicates the existence of an emotion according to the representation of Plutchik. However, this method suffers from ambiguity when the emotion is presented with its opposite, for example the binary classification in a multi-label context can indicate *joy* and *sadness* at the same time, an impossible representation by Plutchik's theory.

The authors Felbo et al. (2017) used transfer learning (Bengio, 2012), which does not require access to the original dataset, but only to the model of an already trained deep learning classifier. This allowed them to classify *sarcasm* (Gal and Ghahramani, 2016) and the 7 emotions of the PsychExp dataset (Wallbott and Scherer, 1986). Others works using transfer learning (Barbieri et al., 2018; Gee and Wang, 2018; Park et al., 2018) demonstrated a great performance in detecting emojis in shared tasks such as SemEval[1].

[1](International Workshop on Semantic Evaluation)

The authors Barbieri et al. (2017) studied the relationship between words and emoticons. They also proposed an approach to predict the most likely emoji associated with a tweet. This proposed approach was based on a Bidirectional Long Short-Term Memory (BiLSTM) architecture (*BiLSTM*).

Zhong and Miao (2019) used a model that extends the Recurrent Convolutional Neural Network (RCNN) using finely-tuned external word representations and DeepMoji phrase representations on the emotion detection task in *SemEval-2019*.

Other work (Tang et al., 2014) proposed a method to learn to incorporate specific words in Word Embeddings and showed an improvement in the performance especially when combining other sets of existing features.

In our knowledge, none of the previous works considered the case of texts with conflicting emotions, hence the need for such a model.

3.2. Datasets Overview

In this section, we present the existing emotional English datasets in chronological order.

The dataset ISEAR, published by (Scherer and Wallbott, 1994) uses the responses of people from different cultures to questionnaires in social media. The final dataset contains about 3,000 reports, for 7,665 sentences labeled with unique emotions. The set uses the labels "joy", "fear", "anger", "sadness", "disgust", "shame" and "guilt".

The WordNet-Affect Lexicon (Valitutti, 2004) is a collection of emotion related words (nouns, verbs, adjectives, and adverbs), classified as "Positive", "Negative", "Neutral", or "Ambiguous", and categorized into 28 subcategories ("Joy", "Love", "Fear", etc.).

The dataset Tales, published by Alm et al. (2005; Bostan and Klinger (2018) is based on literature and consists of 15,302 sentences, with its annotators only agreeing on 1,280 sentences. The goal of this resource is to help build emotion classifiers for literature. The annotation scheme includes Ekman's six basic emotions. Labels 'angry' and 'disgust' are merged.

The dataset AffectiveText, published by Strapparava and Mihalcea (2007; Bostan and Klinger (2018), is built from news headlines. The main objective of this resource is the classification of emotions and valence in news headlines using the basic emotions of Ekman, supplemented by enumerate valence between 0 to 100.

The dataset Blogs, published by Aman and Szpakowicz (2007), includes 5,205 sentences. Each instance annotated with one label. The used annotation scheme corresponds to Ekman's six fundamental emotions.

The dataset EmoTxt , published by Ortu et al. (2015), includes 4000 comments posted by software developers. This corpus contains sentences manually labelled with the emotions "Love", "Joy", "Surprise", "Anger", "Sadness" and "Fear".
The dataset Electoral-Tweets, published by Mohammad and Kiritchenko (2015) for the field of elections, contains more than 100,000 responses to two detailed online questionnaires (questions focused on the emotions, purpose, and style of the electoral tweets). These tweets are annotated via Crowdsourcing and the labels for emotions are non-standard, examples: polite,impolite . The tweets are annotated with emotional words (Bostan and Klinger, 2018).
The dataset Emotion-Stimulus, published by Ghazi et al. (2015), contains 820 sentences that are annotated with both emotions and their causes, and 1,549 sentences that are uniquely marked with emotions. The annotators used FrameNet (Fillmore et al., 2003) to annotate this dataset using the Ekman's theory alimented with the Shame label.
The dataset fb-valence-eveal, published by Preoţiuc-Pietro et al. (2016), is a data set of 2,895 Social Media posts rated by two psychologically-trained annotators on two separate ordinal nine-point scales. These scales represent valence (or sentiment) and arousal (or intensity), which defines each post's position on the circumplex model of affect, a well-established system for describing emotional states.
The dataset Grounded-Emotions, published by Bostan and Klinger (2018), is built on tweets and contains 2,557 instances published by 1,369 users. The labels is "happy" and "sad". The tweets are annotated by the authors.
The dataset TEC, published by Mohammad et al. (2013)(Bostan and Klinger, 2018), includes 21,051 tweets. The main objective of this resource is to use emotion word hashtags as a source of annotation for emotions. The annotation scheme corresponds to Ekman's basic emotion model. They collected tweets with hashtags corresponding to Ekman's six basics emotions: anger, disgust, fear, happy, sadness, and surprise.
The dataset DailyDialogs, published by Li et al. (2017), is based on conversations and includes 13,118 sentences. The annotation used is from Ekman, with a label of "no emotion". A single label by utterance via an expert annotation. This dataset contains annotations about the user's intent and the topic of the dialog.
The dataset EmoBank, published by Buechel and Hahn (2017), is based on several genres and domains. It consists of 10,548 sentences, each one annotated manually according to the emotion expressed by the author and the readers.
The dataset EmoInt, published by Mohammad and Bravo-Marquez (2017) (Bostan and Klinger, 2018), consists of 7,097 tweets. It associates each text with different intensities of emotion. The tweets are annotated via crowdsourcing with intensities of anger, joy, sadness, and fear.
As the previous list shows, there exist many emotional data set to work with. However, they all have the following limitations with regards to Plutchik's theory : 1) The labels are not based on the fundamental emotions of Plutchik's theory; 2) the size of the data may be too small to train an efficient emotion detection model.
Plutchik's theory offers many advantages for the detection of complex emotions. 24 complex emotions can be modeled with just 8 basic emotions; while, the model proposed by Ekman offers 16 complex emotions, and needs a larger data set for its implementation(Ekman, 2004). Our motivation in the present research is to use the Plutchik's theory for the detection of basic and complex emotions. For this purpose, a new dataset was constructed and annotated with the complex emotions.

4. The Proposed Approach

Our ultimate goal is to create an emotion classifier that is capable of detecting complex emotions based on the Plutchik model, and that introduces an implicite rule to handle conflicting emotion representations. This rule forces the classifier to detect either an emotion like joy or sadness but not both at the same time.
The overall process is summarized in Figure 1 and consists in three phases :

(1) collection of annotated data to construct a training annotated corpus from several types of corpora in order to cover the eight basic labels of the Plutchik theory;

(2) detection of basic emotions and representation with a four-dimensional emotion vector. The proposed strategy for the emotion detection relies on multi-label classification using transfer learning (Felbo et al., 2017);

(3) learning and interpretation of complex emotions using multi-label classification.

4.1. Corpus Construction

Our training corpus combines several English data sets from different sources. Table 2 represents the details of the source and types of labels considered. As the table shows, all eight basic emotions according to Plutchik's theory are considered, plus three complex emotions that are generally associated with our model. For instance, we break down complex emotions *Love* into the basic emotions *Trust* and *Joy* in the whole corpus. By repeated the operation for all complex emotions, the initial corpus becomes a multi-label one. Table 2 shows the different corpora, as components of the data set used in this research to detect the basic and complex emotions. These corpora are described in the following paragraphs.

Dataset	Labels
EmoTxt [1]	joy, anger, sadness, love, surprise, fear
PsychExp [2]	joy, fear, anger, sadness, disgust, shame, guilt
DailyDialog [3]	no emotion, anger, disgust, fear, happiness, sadness, surprise
NRC_Emotion_Lexicon_ v0.92 [4] emotion_proposition_store [5]	joy, fear, disgust, anger, sadness, surprise, trust and anticipation
WordNet-Affect (Valitutti, 2004)	joy, fear, disgust, anger, sadness, surprise, trust and anticipation

Table 2: Sources of each component of the data set

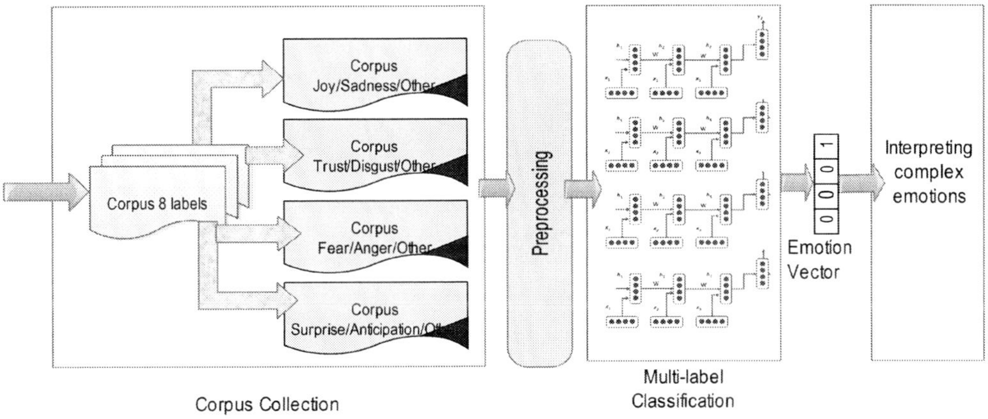

Figure 1: General presentation of the proposed method

Dailydialog (Li et al., 2017) is annotated with the Big Six emotions of Ekman, and it is a multi-turn corpus built for human dialogue. We extracted sentences containing between 5 and 12 words, and deleted the sentences that do not contain emotions in the big Six of Ekman, since they can have emotions that can be represented by the Plutchik model but are absent in Ekman model.
Wordnet samples will help us generate the missing labels in other corpora such as Surprise and Anticipation. In addition, we enriched our corpus with the sources of WordNet and WordNet-Affect (Valitutti, 2004) as follows:
First, we have extracted all the effective examples of WordNet that have a word-annotated relationship in WordNet-Affect. Second, we manually annotated the examples using Crowdsourcing, three users chose emotions that correspond to the 8 basic plutchik emotions.
Then,we choose only the examples to the three evaluators agree on the same emotions.

Word	Examples	label WordNet-Affect
love	She loves her boss and works hard for him	Joy + Trust
love	he has a very complicated love life	Joy + Trust
sad	feeling sad because his dog had died	Sadness
surprise	The news really surprised me	Surprise

Table 3: Examples of annotated WordNet data where the three annotators agreed

Table 3 presents some examples where all of the annotators agreed on the same label.
Table 4 presents the complex emotions that exist in our corpus and that we replaced by the corresponding basic emotions in the Plutchik model. *Love* represents the Primary Dyads, *Guilt* represents Secondary Dyads, and *Shame* represents Tertiary Dyads. Moreover, we augmented our corpus with words associated with the emotions extracted from Wordnet-Affect. Thus, all examples associated with these words have the same affect. Hence, the emotions associated with these words reflect the emotions already present in the examples used in Wordnet.

Complex emotion	Basic emotion	Composition type
Love	Joy + Trust	Primary Dyads
Guilt	Fear + Joy	Secondary Dyads
Shame	Fear + Disgust	Tertiary Dyads

Table 4: Decomposition of complex emotions

The corpus is divided into four sub corpora, each one making use of three labels for emotion representation, its opposite and the absence of the two (e.g., Joy/Sadness/No, Anticipation/Surprise/No, Disgust/Trust/No, Anger/Fear/No). then, The instances of each sub corpus are mixed randomly. We divided each sub-corpus into three parts related to: (1) training 70%, (2) development 15% and (3) testing 15%. We used the same validation process as the one used for DeepMoji (Felbo et al., 2017), using the provided code [2]. The DeepMoji model uses an embedding layer of 256 dimensions to represent each word in a vector space model. A hyperbolic tangent activation function is used to enforce a constraint of each embedding dimension being within [-1, 1]. To capture the context of each word, DeepMoji uses two bidirectional LSTM layers with 1024 hidden units in each (512 in each direction). Finally, the attention mechanism lets the model decide the importance of each word for the prediction task by the projection on 64 outputs of emojis. Our model uses the same architecture with changing the output layer to 3 outputs.

The test phase is done after the generation of the final model. Table 5 represents the statistics by the average number of words per sentence for each label that exist in the corpus. Figure 2 illustrates the distribution of the eight emotions in our corpus by percent.

[1]https://github.com/collab-uniba/EMTk
[2]https://github.com/bfelbo/DeepMoji/tree/master/data
[3]http://yanran.li/dailydialog
[4]Lexicon of the NRC Word Emotion Association.
[5]https://github.com/sebastianruder/emotion_proposition_store

[2]https://github.com/huggingface/torchMoji

Emotion sub data	Train	Eval	Test	Total	Average Sentence Length
Anticipation	1572	336	336	2246	6.1
Joy	5640	1208	1208	8058	6.7
Trust	1653	354	354	1653	7.1
Fear	5859	1255	1255	8370	7.3
Surprise	1317	282	282	1881	6.2
Sadness	3357	719	719	4795	7.4
Disgust	4067	871	871	5810	7.2
Anger	2231	478	478	3188	6.9

Table 5: Statistics by number of labels in the corpus

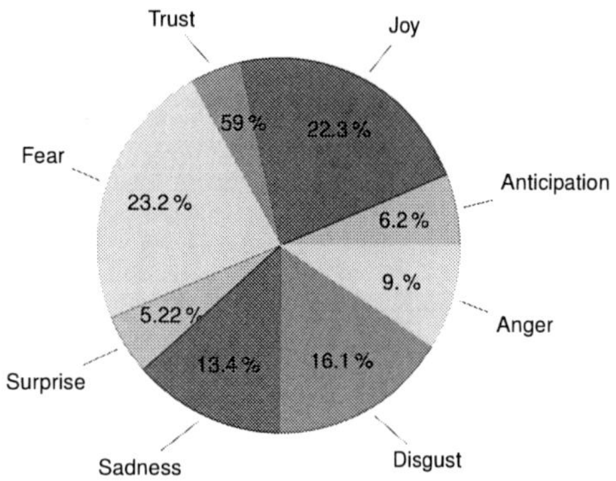

Figure 2: Distribution of emotions in the corpus

4.2. Using the corpus for emotions detection

In the case of the presence of the emotion, we mark 1 and in the case of the presence of the opposite emotion, we mark -1. If the emotion with its inverse are absent we mark 0. Our main objective is to avoid having an emotion with its opposite at the same time, either 1 or -1. In addition, if the model detects 0, then we have no emotion.

With the proposed corpus, the emotion recognition problem can be seen as a problem of learning multi-labels where each of the four dimensions is represented by a label with three values (1,0,-1), each label detected by a Sequence to Vector model (Seq2vec). The seq2vec model used is DeepMoji, as shown in figure 3.

To detect each label, we use transfer learning of a DeepMoji model shown in the figure 3.

DeepMoji model is learnt on 50,000 words of inputs and 65 outputs that correspond to emojis. The model contains two BiLSTM layers that can learn the sequential structure of the sentence. These two layers were kept during the transfer learning. On the other hand, the layers of the attention and the output are replaced by a layer of three outputs.

Our modelling of emotional states is based on representing of emotional states in the form of vectors. For each emotional state, there is a vector in a 4-dimensional space, each dimension representing a pair of contradictory basic emotions (eg. Joy and Sadness and No).

We propose to use the same basic emotions of the Plutchik model to define the dimensions of our base. Therefore, the number of dimensions of our basic emotion is four pairs of emotions and is formally defined by the base B = ((Joy, Sadness), (Trust, Disgust), (Fear, Anger), (Surprise, Anticipation)). Thus, any emotion can be realized using a combination of the other fundamental emotions that define our base B. Our model represents the following axes, as defined in Table 6:

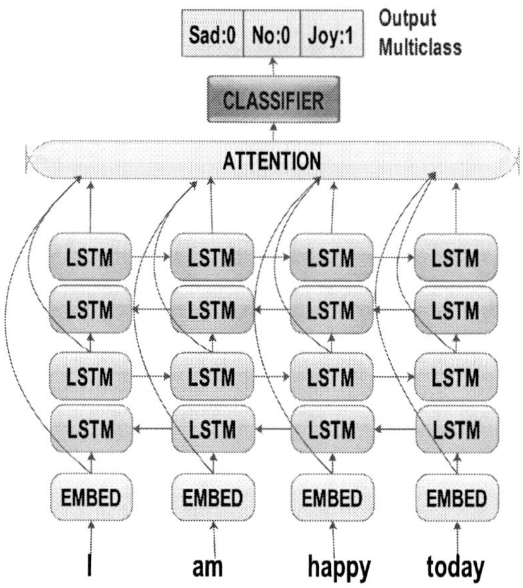

Figure 3: The architecture used to transfer learning based on the DeepMoji model for each classifier multiclass.

Positive axis(+)	Negative axis(-)
Joy	Sadness
Trust	Disgust
Fear	Anger
Surprise	Anticipation

Table 6: Combinations of two by two conflicting emotions in 4 dimensions

Each basic positive emotion is in the interval [0,1] and every basic negative emotion is in the interval [-1,0].

This allows on the one hand to represent an infinite number of complex emotions, because our model is a continuous one, and on the other hand, to offer high-performance mathematical tools for the analysis and processing of these emotions.

4.3. Learning complex emotions

Table 8 shows a representation of primary complex emotions using the Plutchik model, with the combinations of 2 adjacent emotions separated by no emotion constituting the primary dyads.

Table 7 shows a representation in 8 dimensions equivalent to Table 8. The latter represents the emotion in 4 dimensions and prevents the representation of the emotion with his inverse that will serve as a transition matrix W to detect the main complex emotions.

The numerical contents of Table 8 are used as a transition matrix W to detect complex emotions for primary dyads. To this end, we converted each type of dyad in table 1 into a W transition matrix.

Complex emotions Primary Dyad	Anticipation	Joy	Trust	Fear	Surprise	Sadness	Disgust	Anger
Optimism	1	1	0	0	0	0	0	0
Love	0	1	1	0	0	0	0	0
Submission	0	0	1	1	0	0	0	0
Apprehension	0	0	0	1	1	0	0	0
Disappointment	0	0	0	0	1	1	0	0
Remorse	0	0	0	0	0	1	1	0
Contempt	0	0	0	0	0	0	1	1
Aggressiveness	1	0	0	0	0	0	0	1

Table 7: Combinations of 2 adjacent emotions that make the primary dyads in 8 dimensions.

Complex emotions Primary Dyad	Anticipation-Surprise	Joy-Sadness	Trust-Disgust	Fear-Anger
Optimism	1	1	0	0
Love	0	1	1	0
Submission	0	0	1	1
Apprehension	-1	0	0	1
Disappointment	-1	-1	0	0
Remord	0	-1	-1	0
Contempt	0	0	-1	-1
Aggressiveness	1	0	0	-1

Table 8: Combinations of 2 adjacent emotions that make the primary dyads in 4 dimensions.

Equations 1 and 2 show how one can detect the presence of a complex emotion by multiplying matrix W by the vector V that represents the emotion coordinates in our vector space (equation 1).

$$\underset{Primary\ Dyad}{S} = \underset{Primary\ Dyad}{W} \quad V = \begin{bmatrix} 1 & 1 & 0 & 0 \\ 0 & 1 & 1 & 0 \\ 0 & 0 & 1 & 1 \\ -1 & 0 & 0 & 1 \\ -1 & -1 & 0 & 0 \\ 0 & -1 & -1 & 0 \\ 0 & 0 & -1 & -1 \\ 1 & 0 & 0 & -1 \end{bmatrix} \begin{bmatrix} a \\ b \\ c \\ d \end{bmatrix} \quad (1)$$

The result for the complex emotion obtained should be the result that maximizes a component of the vectors. A problem that can be faced is that the components can exceed the value 1. To fix this problem, we propose to seek the value greater than 1. Does it mean to convey that no complex emotion is detected when $S_i < 1$.

Equation 2 presents our objective function for reading the complex emotion. The complex emotions generated by the index i correspond to the emotions in the transition matrix W given in table 8.

$$\begin{cases} \hat{Emotion\ complex} = \underset{i}{argmax}(S_i) \\ and \\ S_i \geq 1 \end{cases} \quad (2)$$

i∈ (*Optimism* =0, *Love* =1, *Submission* =2, *Alarm*=3, *Disappointment*=4,*Contemptment*=5, *Remord*=6, *Aggressiveness*=7)

5. Experiments and Results

We conducted two sets of experiments. The first experiments considered the emotion space in four dimensions, each one having three labels that reflect the presence of an emotion and its inverse, or the absence of both. As a result, the classifiers consider the vector of four labels: *Joy/Sadness/No* , *Trust/Disgust/No*, *Anticipation/Surprise/No*, *Anger/Fear/No*.

The second experiments turn the problem into binary classification, we modeled as the baseline approach. This method, called the binary relevance method, models the emotion space in 8 dimensions, each one having two classes that reflect the presence of emotion and its absence. Thus, The classifiers consider the vector of 8 labels: *Joy/No ,Sadness/No*, *Trust/No*, *Disgust/No*, *Anticipation/No*, *Surprise/No*, *Anger/No*, *Fear/No*.

Both sets of experiments are based on transfer learning and can be represented by table 9.

Model	Axis Emotions	Recall	Precision	F1	Macro F1	Exact Match
Our Model in 4 dimensions space	joy/sadness/No	0.56	0.44	**0.49**	**0.54**	**0.43**
	anger/fear/No	0.61	0.56	**0.58**		
	surprise/anticip/No	0.55	0.51	**0.52**		
	trust/disgust/No	0.63	0.59	**0.57**		
Our Model in 8 dimensions space	joy/No	0.48	0.41	0.44	0.46	0.23
	sadness/No	0.46	0.39	0.42		
	anger/No	0.51	0.47	0.48		
	fear/No	0.52	0.44	0.47		
	surprise/No	0.46	0.42	0.43		
	anticipation/No	0.45	0.39	0.41		
	trust/No	0.54	0.49	0.51		
	disgust/No	0.57	0.48	0.52		

Table 9: Results based on precision, recall, F-score for different classifications after using transfer learning.

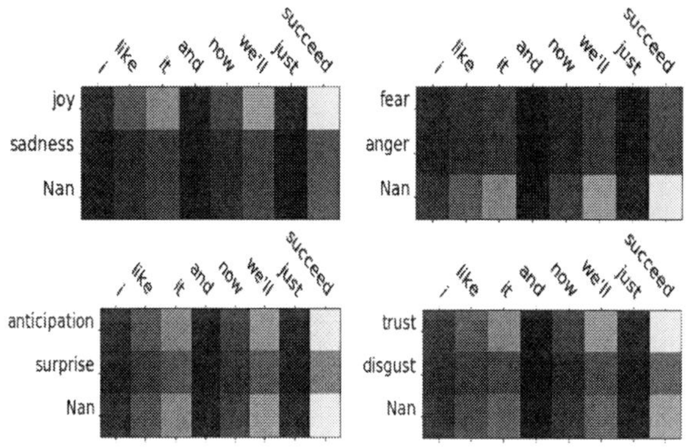

Figure 4: Visualization of the attention for each Multi Class classifier with example '*I like it and now we'll just succeed*'.

Table 9 provides the obtained Precision, Recall, F1 and Macro-F1 values of the model trained with transfer learning, comparing the use four-dimensional space and eight-dimensional space representations.

Figure 4 illustrates four attentions, each one detected by one classifier. They represent the score of participation of each word in the example above, with the model detecting the associated class. The yellow color represents a high probability of contribution, whereas the blue color represents a low probability of contribution. The classifiers *Joy/Sadness* and *anticipation/surprise* identified the labels *Joy*, *Trust* and *Anticipation*. The classifiers represent the absence of other emotions with the label *Nan*. The complex emotion detected in this example is *Optimism*, *Fatalism*, and *Love*, as *Joy+Anticipation=Optimism,Trust+Anticipation=Fatalism* and Joy+Trust=Love.

5.1. Comparison with other models

As our model appears to be the first to apply the Plutchik model to a text with conflicting emotions, a precise comparison with other works is not possible. However, as there exit methods that attempt to detect complex emotions by direct means directly such as PsychExp and EmoTxt, a qualitative comparison may give insight into the strengths and weaknesses of the different methods.

Model	Complex Emotion	Average-F1	Exact Match
Our Model	Love (Joy + Trust)	**0.58**	0.52
	Shame (Fear + Disgust)	**0.54**	0.53
	Guilt (Fear + Joy)	**0.54**	0.51
Model	Complex Emotion	F1	Accuracy
DeepMoji(**PsychExp**)	Shame	0.56	**0.59**
	Guilt	**0.54**	**0.60**
DeepMoji (**PsychExp + EmoTxt**)	Love	0.57	**0.63**
	Shame	0.53	**0.58**
	Guilt	0.51	**0.58**

Table 10: Results based on Exact Match, F-score for Love, Guilt and, Shame classification after using Transfer Learning.

Table 10 presents a comparison with the state of the art, which uses public data sets that contain some complex emotions. The *EmoTxt* dataset contains a test with 200 instances of the labels '*Love*' and the PsychExp dataset contains a test with 264 and 427 instances of labels *Guilt* and *Shame*, respectively.

For the first model, we used the DeepMoji model (Felbo et al., 2017) with the *PsychExp* data set, and for the second, we added the *Love* label to the model after training it with *PsychExp* and *EmoTxt* dataset. The *Love* label represents the *Joy* + *Trust* detection found in the Primary Dyads. The *Shame* label represents the '*Fear* + *Disgust*' detection found in the Tertiary Dyads. The *Guilt* label represents the '*Fear* + *Joy*' detection that is in the Secondary Dyads.

6. Discussion

The analysis of our experiments, we notice a correlation between the different loss estimates illustrated in figure 5. An inverse relationship can be detected between the loss and the results shown in table 9: the more we reduce the loss the more we increase the F1 score. In addition, we can notice that the duration of learning depends on the size of the data. Moreover, the convergence towards the local minima collapses quickly, because the DeepMoji parameters used are using Transfer Learning.

The obtained results also reveal a slight difference between the different experiments in table 10. Indeed, the average F1 score of our model for label *Guilt (Fear + Joy)* is greater then the F1 score of the experiment done by the DeepMoji model (PsychExp), but the DeepMoji model accuracy exceeds the Exact match (subset accuracy) of our model by 0.07, because the exact match means that both labels detect it at the same time.

Our model has a better performance in terms of average F1 score for the label *Love (Trust + Joy)* when compared to the DeepMoji model (PsychExp + EmoTxt) which contains the *love* label. However, the accuracy of DeepMoji (PsychExp + EmoTxt) is better than the Exact match of our model.

Table 9 also reveals obvious difference between models. The F1-score in the experiment *Joy/Sadness* improves to 5% (from 0.44 to 0.49) due to the incorporation of the reverse emotions rule, which imposes that the presence of an emotion excludes the existence of its inverse.

Figures 6b and 6a are attention heat maps for two sentences. The first one is an affirmative sentence, '*I am happy*', and it is classified by the label Joy; the second one, ' textit I am not happy', is its negative sentence and is classified by the label Sadness.

The classifiers detect the labels (Sadness, Joy) through the yellow boxes. The words that caused the detection of sadness are '*not happy*' and the word that caused the detection of joy is '*happy*'. However, the word '*I*' participates less in the generation of emotion, this can be explained by the fact that the words '*happy*' and '*not happy*' are subjective words. The word '*am*' has a weak intensity represented by the blue box. It does not contribute to the generation of the emotion, because it is objective and can be replaced by another entity without affecting the subjectivity of the sentence.

The comparison between the attentions of the figures 6b and 6a illustrates the independence of the emotion from the vocabulary. The replacement of the sentence '*I am happy*' by '*I am not happy*' shows that the system learnt an interesting rule as follows: the reversal of sentences by negation involves the reversal of the *Joy* emotion by the *Sadness* emotion.

The labels *Love*, *Guilt*, and *Shame* in Table 10 represent the detection of Primary Dyads, Secondary Dyads, and Tertiary Dyads, which confirms that our hypothesis worked well on these three test labels with a Macro-F1 exceeding 50%.

7. Conclusions and perspectives

This paper presents a novel approach for the detection of complex emotions, according to the Plutchik model and using multi-label classifiers. These classifiers are divided into 4 multiclass classifiers. Our main contributions are listed as follows:

(1) A new corpus labeled by the 8 basic emotions of Plutchik.

(2) Representation of complex emotions according to the Plutchik theory, in a vector space with four axes.

(3) Learning new rules that the detected emotions do not show up using their inverse emotions in the same axis.

To our knowledge, there exist no previous efforts to automatically detect and recognize complex emotions which was introduced by Plutchik's theory, in a textual data using four dimensions and deep neural networks.

Our proposed research is a crucial step towards building a conversational agent endowed with emotional intelligence. We are also looking forward to transferring the idea of complex emotions to task-oriented dialogs and multi-turn dialog generation problems.

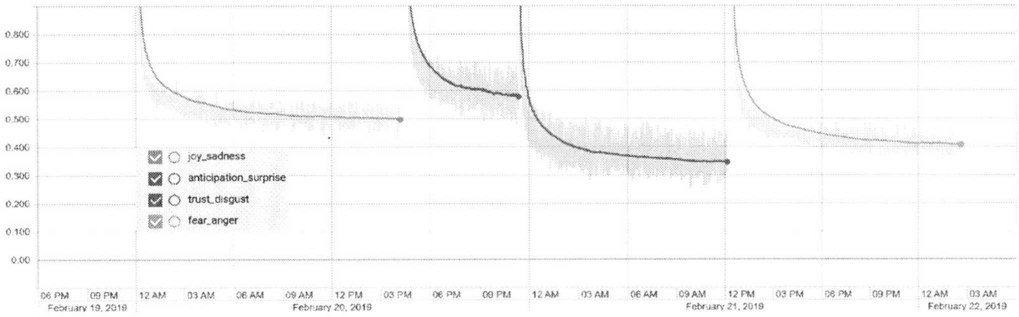

Figure 5: Visualization of loss reduction for each classifier Multi Class in evaluation process.

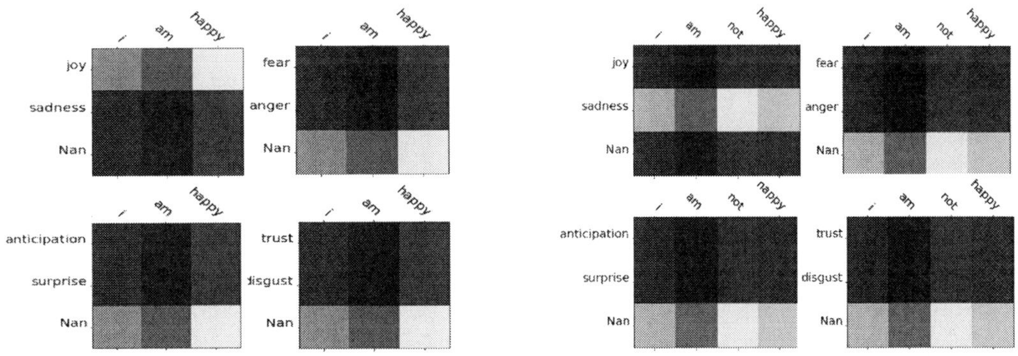

(a) Visualization of the attention for example '*I am happy*' (b) Visualization of the attention for example '*I am not happy*'.

Figure 6: Visualization of the attention mechanism.

8. Bibliography

Alm, C. O., Roth, D., and Sproat, R. (2005). Emotions from text: Machine learning for text-based emotion prediction. In *Proceedings of the Conference on Human Language Technology and Empirical Methods in Natural Language Processing*, HLT '05, pages 579–586, Stroudsburg, PA, USA. Association for Computational Linguistics.

Aman, S. and Szpakowicz, S. (2007). Identifying expressions of emotion in text. In *International Conference on Text, Speech and Dialogue*, pages 196–205. Springer.

Barbieri, F., Ballesteros, M., and Saggion, H. (2017). Are emojis predictable? *CoRR*, abs/1702.07285.

Barbieri, F., Camacho-Collados, J., Ronzano, F., Anke, L. E., Ballesteros, M., Basile, V., Patti, V., and Saggion, H. (2018). Semeval 2018 task 2: Multilingual emoji prediction. In *Proceedings of The 12th International Workshop on Semantic Evaluation*, pages 24–33.

Bengio, Y. (2012). Deep learning of representations for unsupervised and transfer learning. In *Proceedings of ICML Workshop on Unsupervised and Transfer Learning*, pages 17–36.

Bostan, L.-A.-M. and Klinger, R. (2018). An analysis of annotated corpora for emotion classification in text. In *Proceedings of the 27th International Conference on Computational Linguistics*, pages 2104–2119, Santa Fe, New Mexico, USA, August. Association for Computational Linguistics.

Buechel, S. and Hahn, U. (2017). EmoBank: Studying the impact of annotation perspective and representation format on dimensional emotion analysis. In *Proceedings of the 15th Conference of the European Chapter of the Association for Computational Linguistics: Volume 2, Short Papers*, pages 578–585, Valencia, Spain, April. Association for Computational Linguistics.

De Bonis, M. (1996). *Connaître les émotions humaines*, volume 212. Editions Mardaga.

Ekman, P. (2004). What we become emotional about. In *Feelings and emotions. The Amsterdam symposium*, pages 119–135.

Felbo, B., Mislove, A., Søgaard, A., Rahwan, I., and Lehmann, S. (2017). Using millions of emoji occurrences to learn any-domain representations for detecting sentiment, emotion and sarcasm. pages 1615–1625, September.

Fillmore, C. J., Johnson, C. R., and Petruck, M. R. (2003). Background to framenet. *International journal of lexicography*, 16(3):235–250.

Gal, Y. and Ghahramani, Z. (2016). A theoretically grounded application of dropout in recurrent neural networks. In *Advances in neural information processing systems*, pages 1019–1027.

Gee, G. and Wang, E. (2018). psyml at semeval-2018 task 1: Transfer learning for sentiment and emotion analysis. In *Proceedings of The 12th International Workshop on Semantic Evaluation*, pages 369–376.

Ghazi, D., Inkpen, D., and Szpakowicz, S. (2015). Detecting emotion stimuli in emotion-bearing sentences. In Alexander Gelbukh, editor, *Computational Linguistics and Intelligent Text Processing*, pages 152–165, Cham. Springer International Publishing.

Kunneman, F., Liebrecht, C., and van den Bosch, A. (2014). The (un) predictability of emotional hashtags in twitter. In *Proceedings of the 5th Workshop on Language Analysis for Social Media (LASM)*, pages 26–34.

Li, Y., Su, H., Shen, X., Li, W., Cao, Z., and Niu, S. (2017). Dailydialog: A manually labelled multi-turn dialogue dataset. In *Proceedings of The 8th International Joint Conference on Natural Language Processing (IJCNLP 2017)*.

Mohammad, S. M. and Bravo-Marquez, F. (2017). Emotion intensities in tweets. *CoRR*, abs/1708.03696.

Mohammad, S. M. and Kiritchenko, S. (2015). Using hashtags to capture fine emotion categories from tweets. *Computational Intelligence*, 31(2):301–326.

Mohammad, S. M., Kiritchenko, S., and Zhu, X. (2013). Nrc-canada: Building the state-of-the-art in sentiment analysis of tweets. *arXiv preprint arXiv:1308.6242*.

Nakov, P., Ritter, A., Rosenthal, S., Sebastiani, F., and Stoyanov, V. (2016). Semeval-2016 task 4: Sentiment analysis in twitter. In *Proceedings of the 10th international workshop on semantic evaluation (semeval-2016)*, pages 1–18.

Nida, H., Mahira, K., Mudasir, M., Mudasir Ahmed, M., and Mohsin, M. (2019). Automatic emotion classifier. In Bibudhendu Pati, et al., editors, *Progress in Advanced Computing and Intelligent Engineering*, pages 565–572, Singapore. Springer Singapore.

Nikhil, N. and Srivastava, M. M. (2018). Binarizer at semeval-2018 task 3: Parsing dependency and deep learning for irony detection. *CoRR*, abs/1805.01112.

Ortu, M., Adams, B., Destefanis, G., Tourani, P., Marchesi, M., and Tonelli, R. (2015). Are bullies more productive? empirical study of affectiveness vs. issue fixing time. In *2015 IEEE/ACM 12th Working Conference on Mining Software Repositories*, pages 303–313. IEEE.

Park, J. H., Xu, P., and Fung, P. (2018). Plusemo2vec at semeval-2018 task 1: Exploiting emotion knowledge from emoji and# hashtags. *arXiv preprint arXiv:1804.08280*.

Plutchik, R. (1980). Emotion: A psychoevolutionary analysis. *Nueva York: Harper and Row*.

Plutchik, R. (2003). *Emotions and life: Perspectives from psychology, biology, and evolution.* American Psychological Association.

Posner, J., Russell, J. A., and Peterson, B. S. (2005). The circumplex model of affect: An integrative approach to affective neuroscience, cognitive development, and psychopathology. *Development and Psychopathology*, 17(3):715–734.

Preoţiuc-Pietro, D., Schwartz, H. A., Park, G., Eichstaedt, J., Kern, M., Ungar, L., and Shulman, E. (2016). Modelling valence and arousal in facebook posts. In *Proceedings of the 7th Workshop on Computational Approaches to Subjectivity, Sentiment and Social Media Analysis*, pages 9–15.

Read, J. (2005). Using emoticons to reduce dependency in machine learning techniques for sentiment classification. In *Proceedings of the ACL student research workshop*, pages 43–48.

Scherer, K. R. and Wallbott, H. G. (1994). Evidence for universality and cultural variation of differential emotion response patterning. *Journal of personality and social psychology*, 66(2):310.

Strapparava, C. and Mihalcea, R. (2007). Semeval-2007 task 14: Affective text. In *Proceedings of the Fourth International Workshop on Semantic Evaluations (SemEval-2007)*, pages 70–74.

Suttles, J. and Ide, N. (2013). Distant supervision for emotion classification with discrete binary values. In Alexander Gelbukh, editor, *Computational Linguistics and Intelligent Text Processing*, pages 121–136, Berlin, Heidelberg. Springer Berlin Heidelberg.

Tang, D., Wei, F., Yang, N., Zhou, M., Liu, T., and Qin, B. (2014). Learning sentiment-specific word embedding for twitter sentiment classification. In *Proceedings of the 52nd Annual Meeting of the Association for Computational Linguistics (Volume 1: Long Papers)*, volume 1, pages 1555–1565.

Valitutti, R. (2004). Wordnet-affect: an affective extension of wordnet. In *In Proceedings of the 4th International Conference on Language Resources and Evaluation*, pages 1083–1086.

Wallbott, H. G. and Scherer, K. R. (1986). How universal and specific is emotional experience? evidence from 27 countries on five continents. *Information (International Social Science Council)*, 25(4):763–795.

Yang, Z., Yang, D., Dyer, C., He, X., Smola, A., and Hovy, E. (2016). Hierarchical attention networks for document classification. In *Proceedings of the 2016 Conference of the North American Chapter of the Association for Computational Linguistics: Human Language Technologies*, pages 1480–1489.

Zhong, P. and Miao, C. (2019). ntuer at semeval-2019 task 3: Emotion classification with word and sentence representations in rcnn. *arXiv preprint arXiv:1902.07867*.

Workshop on Linguistic and Neurocognitive Resources (LiNCr2020), pages 59–60
Language Resources and Evaluation Conference (LREC 2020), Marseille, 11–16 May 2020

Sensorimotor norms for 506 Russian nouns

Alex Miklashevsky

Potsdam Embodied Cognition Group (PECoG), University of Potsdam, Germany

Embodied cognitive science suggested a number of variables describing our sensorimotor experience associated with different concepts: modality experience rating (i.e., relationship between words and images of a particular perceptive modality – visual, auditory, haptic etc., see Lynott and Connell, 2009; Lynott and Connell, 2013; Lynott et al., 2019), manipulability (the necessity for an object to interact with human hands in order to perform its function), vertical spatial localization. According to the embodied cognition theory, claiming that our bodily experiences underlie abstract thought (see Kiefer and Pulvermüller, 2012; Meteyard et al., 2012; Fischer and Zwaan, 2008, for reviews; also see Barsalou, 2008), these semantic variables capture our mental representations and thus should influence word learning, processing and production. However, it is not clear how these new variables are related to such traditional variables as imageability, age of acquisition (AoA) and word frequency, known to strongly influence word processing. In the presented database, normative data on the modality (visual, auditory, haptic, olfactory, and gustatory) ratings, vertical spatial localization of the object, manipulability, imageability, age of acquisition, and subjective frequency for 506 Russian nouns are collected. Strongest correlations were observed between olfactory and gustatory modalities (.81), visual modality and imageability (.78), haptic modality and manipulability (.7). Other modalities also significantly correlate with imageability: olfactory (.35), gustatory (.24), and haptic (.67). Factor analysis divided variables into four groups where visual and haptic modality ratings were combined with imageability, manipulability and AoA (the first factor); word length, frequency and AoA formed the second factor; olfactory modality was united with gustatory (the third factor); spatial localization only is included in the fourth factor. Importantly, the database includes semantic categories indicated for each word (e.g., food, transport, mental or emotional concepts), thus making comparisons between categories possible. The database is available online together with a publication describing the method of data collection and data parameters (Miklashevsky, 2018).

References

Barsalou, L. W. (2008). Grounded cognition. *Annu. Rev.* Psychol., 59, 617-645.

Fischer, M. H., & Zwaan, R. A. (2008). Embodied language: A review of the role of the motor system in language comprehension. *The Quarterly Journal of Experimental Psychology, 61*(6), 825-850.

Kiefer, M., & Pulvermüller, F. (2012). Conceptual representations in mind and brain: theoretical developments, current evidence and future directions. *Cortex, 48*(7), 805-825.

Lynott, D., & Connell, L. (2009). Modality exclusivity norms for 423 object properties. *Behavior Research Methods, 41*(2), 558-564.

Lynott, D., & Connell, L. (2013). Modality exclusivity norms for 400 nouns: The relationship between perceptual experience and surface word form. *Behavior Research Methods, 45*(2), 516-526.

Lynott, D., Connell, L., Brysbaert, M., Brand, J., & Carney, J. (2019). The Lancaster Sensorimotor Norms: multidimensional measures of perceptual and action strength for 40,000 English words. *Behavior Research Methods*, 1-21.

Meteyard, L., Cuadrado, S. R., Bahrami, B., & Vigliocco, G. (2012). Coming of age: A review of embodiment and the neuroscience of semantics. *Cortex, 48*(7), 788-804.

Miklashevsky, A. (2018). Perceptual experience norms for 506 Russian nouns: Modality rating, spatial localization, manipulability, imageability and other variables. *Journal of Psycholinguistic Research, 47*(3), 641-661.

Association for Computational Linguistics
209 N. Eighth Street
Stroudsburg, Pennsylvania 18360

ISBN 978-1-7138-1266-1

CURRAN ASSOCIATES INC.
proceedings.com